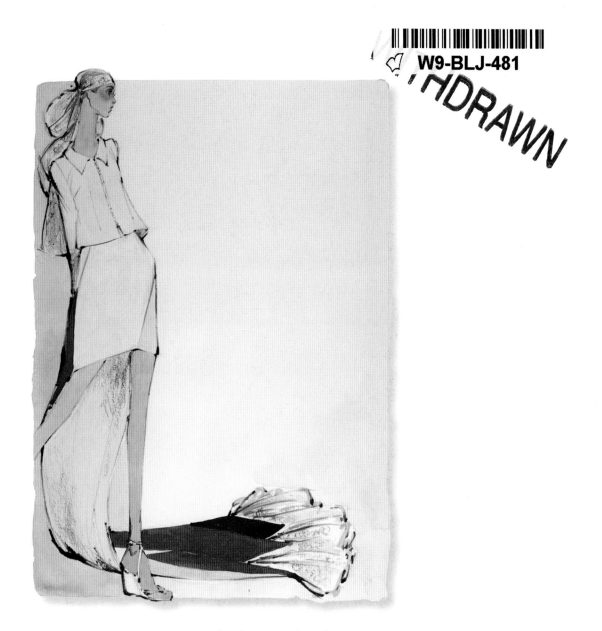

Fashion
Design Course

BARRON'S

STEVEN FAERM

Fashion
Design Course

First edition for North America published in 2010 by Barron's
Educational Series, Inc.

A QUARTO BOOK

Copyright © 2010 Quarto Inc.

All inquiries should be addressed to:
Barron's Educational Series, Inc.
250 Wireless Boulevard
Hauppauge, New York 11788
www.barronseduc.com

ISBN-13: 978-0-7641-4423-3
ISBN-10: 0-7641-4423-5

Library of Congress Control No.: 2009940543

QUAR.FDCO

Conceived, designed, and produced by
Quarto Publishing plc
The Old Brewery
6 Blundell Street
London
N7 9BH

Senior editor: Katie Hallam
Copy editor: Claire Waite-Brown
Art director: Caroline Guest
Art editor: Jackie Palmer
Designer: Simon Brewster
Picture research: Sarah Bell
Creative director: Moira Clinch
Publisher: Paul Carslake

Color separation by Modern Age Repro House Ltd., Hong Kong
Printed in China by 1010 Printing International Limited

9 8 7 6 5 4 3 2 1

Contents

introduction

Learning how to be a successful fashion designer involves understanding a wide variety of core principles. In this book you will learn various methods of designing, how to build a quantitative and qualitative body of research, how to use inspirations in the design process, how fabric knowledge and color principles strengthen a designer's message, and how to evolve your own vision. By mastering these principles you will develop your creativity and refine your understanding of what makes a successful design.

▽ **Positive makes negative** Figure composition, strategic placement of accent color, and interesting negative space make this presentation dynamic. The collection is clearly displayed through mood and figure poses.

▷ **Tones and texture** The sensitive tonal relationships of this color palette serve to underscore the importance of texture in this winter sportswear group. Graphic print gives juxtaposition to the organic shapes and subtle texture.

▽▽ Detail oriented Form, texture, and scale are essential foundations for design and enable this pocket detail to update the most basic garment.

▽ Effective engineering Mastering the principles of garment construction enables designers to break the traditional mold, as seen in this innovative collection.

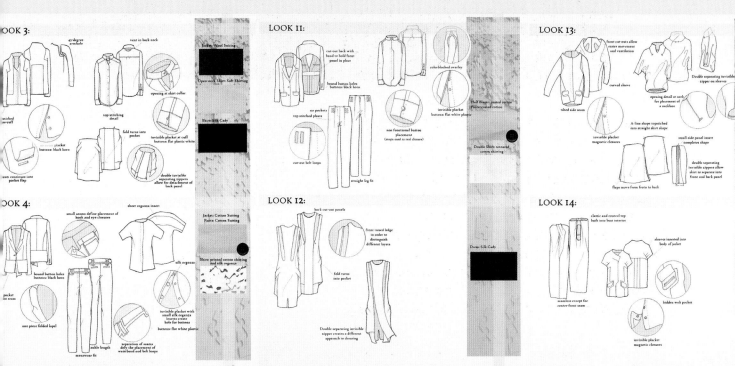

By learning something of the history of fashion design and looking at those exponents who have left an indelible mark, you will acquire a context for the shifts involved in the world of fashion and begin to understand the evolutions and revolutions that have occurred. The branding of fashion and customer identity are also explored, so you will learn how collections are designed around a customer base to remain focused, thereby creating an aspirational product and label.

The core of this book outlines primary design principles that will give you a solid foundation for how to work, considers the fundamental terminologies and design processes, and looks at various approaches to creating work through challenging assignments. By exposing yourself to new methodologies of design in your development, you will acquire versatility of approach and learn about the frameworks that give you utmost creativity.

This coursebook finishes with a full preparation for the professional world by discussing types of portfolio presentations, how to create a stellar résumé, tips for interviewing, and the many career possibilities related to acquiring a working knowledge of fashion design.

This coursebook also includes interviews with industry leaders who provide contextual information about the industry, the profession, what makes great design, and how to prepare as a future designer in today's fast-evolving world.

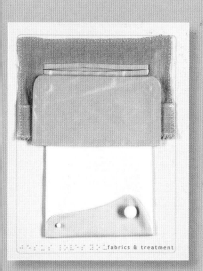

UNIT 1
being a fashion designer

How do we define great fashion design? How do designers create work that stimulates consumer desire, advances the context of fashion design, and ultimately leaves a thumbprint on our culture?

▽ **Design purity** Successful fashion is never meek in the message a designer wishes to communicate. Inspired by the hand movements for massage, this collection uses form and materials to capture ideas of movement and pressure.

The way designers approach their design process is a highly personalized road map, but they all share similarities in the principles of fashion design. As creative individuals with voracious appetites for cultural and societal events, designers often call upon a sixth sense that allows them to know what people will want to wear in the seasons to come. They are extremely attuned to historical, cultural, societal, political, and economic changes in the world, and are able to scrutinize pop culture as an anthropologist would. This constant exposure

There are some concepts you must bear in mind when evolving your point of view:

- **Stay focused** Having a focused point of view is essential. Sometimes it isn't the design that's necessarily new, but how it's framed.

- **Be well rounded** The industry demands designers who can create something that is relevant to today and aesthetically in demand, but also who understand the lifestyle and motivations of their consumers.

- **Straddle two worlds** Keep one foot on the market's needs and one foot on your identity as an artist. Designers don't work in a bubble, and need to know where the market may sway, yet they must always remain consistent to their voice to maintain customer loyalty.

- **Build your skills** Broad design knowledge and vocabulary will allow you to solve problems with whichever techniques will be most successful. Design is, on some levels, problem solving.

- **Keep up with new technologies** Often new materials and methods of production are developed for other purposes, then reappropriated by the fashion world to create new contexts and innovations in fashion design.

- **Understand relevancy** Maintain a high degree of content and context in your work through historical, cultural, societal, political, and economic observations.

- **Exercise your creative muscles** Explore the different methods in creating collections, the types of inspirations and materials used, contexts and usage, and even customer parameters.

- **Have a pure vision** Strive for your designs to always be nonreferential to other designers' work. Innovation and having something new to say to the world must be a constant goal.

NANAE TAKATA

and ability to synthesize research lets designers predict consciously and subconsciously which colors will be favored, which type of silhouette and mood will prevail, how the retail experience may evolve, what people will want from fashion, what will motivate their decisions, and what kind of consumer behavior will arise.

Successful designers keep their target audience in mind from season to season, but subtly adapt their approach to keep on par with the current trends and cultural climate. A designer's customers and their lifestyle will always underscore the collection's purpose.

What Is Fashion? What Is Clothing?

Fashion and clothing may appear to be the same thing, but they are far from it. It is essential that you understand the two so that the ideas you put forth are unique, solidify your vision, and strengthen your creative development. They may even challenge accepted norms and perceptions of what fashion design is.

Fashion is

Aspirational
Fantasy
Visionary
Content rich
Contextual
Unadulterated
Saturated in message
Innovative
Challenging
New
Unique
Strong in narrative
Artistic
About advancing design forward

Clothing is

Lacking in identity
Homogenized
Generic
Undefined
Dull
Common
Incoherent
Banal
"Product"
Filtered
Bland
Lacking in specificity

△ **Inspiration interpretation** Inspirations can be suggested or literal, as seen in this example inspired by Russian symbols. The modern silhouette reflects well-researched historical patterns.

△ **Character study** The high level of focus the designer has for the customer provides this grouping with a strong sense of character. Colors, fabrics, treatments, and targeted market all support one another to produce a successful synthesis.

What Fashion Designers Do

There is a range of tasks most designers are involved with on a regular basis. A designer may not be expected to do every one of the activities directly, but their supervision is essential.

A designer is ultimately responsible for the design of each collection as it moves from inspiration through production. Even if designers have a support staff of design assistants, fabric researchers and developers, patternmakers, computer design specialists, and technical designers, they must supervise and direct their design-room team in an appropriate and timely manner.

PRINCIPAL TASKS

- **Perform research** Establish mood and accumulate visual references for collections.
- **Follow trends** Keep up-to-date on design and market trends directly and indirectly related to the field.
- **Create mood/concept boards** Edit research to show a direction and present to retailers and editors for feedback.
- **Source fabrics** International and domestic fabric fairs are an invaluable resource. Establish relationships with local fabric suppliers for ordering samples and production yardage.
- **Gain knowledge of fabrics** Understand factors such as drape, usability, physical performance, aesthetics, cost, effects on production, and yardage minimums required.

△ △ **Developing ideas**
A croquis book is the corner-stone for all design work, enabling idea conception, variety of design, and merchandising from sketches.

△ **Capturing a niche**
The quantity of design aesthetics offered today is unprecedented because of designers' ability to address specific markets, as seen in the work of Matthew Williamson.

▷ **Every little detail**
A high degree of specificity is critical. Garment fit, detail proportion, and design relationships must be clearly specified.

- **Coordinate design** Work with print studios or in-house design staff to develop textile print designs, graphics, and colorways.

- **Monitor quality** Establish color standards and check lab-dip submissions for solid yardage and print development.

- **Develop the collection** Sketch designs, silhouettes, and "looks," and ensure that they can be readily interpreted by patternmakers, drapers, merchandisers, and production specialists.

- **Develop prototype** Work with an in-house sample room; this may involve contributing to the pattern cutting, draping the garments, or both.

- **Resource and select trims** A designer may also design them accordingly.

- **Create merchandise plans**

- **Communicate detailed information** Sketches/writing clarify all aspects of construction and special details via a spec sheet that gives detailed measurements.

- **Conduct/participate in fittings** Provide quick and concise responses to problems in fit and proportion.

- **Communicate with production staff** Visit factories or contractors to direct the execution of the collection and quality standards: Staying up-to-date on technology may inform design.

- **Perform checks** Compare prototypes, samples, and production against specifications (specs).

- **Understand cost** Know the market prices for materials and components—and have a fundamental knowledge of margins (markup) and profitability.

- **Present the collection** Show sales teams, executives, retailers, and media.

Garment "flats" provide an accurate representation of the design

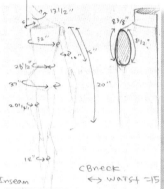

Model's measurements ensure accurate muslin and pattern development

Muslin allows designers to test proportion, fit, and shape before finalizing

Specific knit stitch information is provided for final execution

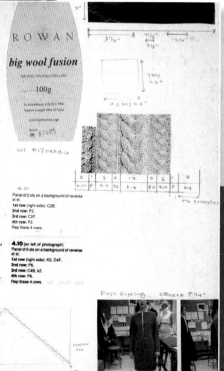

The many hats worn by designers Design isn't just about conceiving and sketching ideas. From development during the croquis process, editing the final selection, and the technical process undertaken when design ideas are tested and refined, designers never stop their critical analysis of what they wish the collection to be.

UNIT 2
history of fashion:
lifestyle and cultural changes

Fashion serves as a thumbprint that society leaves behind, and helps to define an era. It is the barometer of our culture.

Fashion measures people's attitudes, morals, views, and delineations in society, reflects economic status, and creates "tribes" that one aspires to join. It nonverbally communicates information about a person and their affiliations. From the hobble skirts of the early twentieth century, which hindered women's movement, to the fabric restrictions imposed during World War II, to the infusion of street culture in the 1960s, and the dress-to-impress luxury of the 1980s, fashion has represented societal forces and views of the time that then created the impetus for change.

▽ **The manor born** In the early twentieth century, attire communicated one's hierarchy. Garments that required assistance when dressing and hemlines restricting full movement indicate that this group was of the "leisurely" class.

Historical Beginnings

Before the late nineteenth century and the emergence of fashion houses, clothing was largely an "at home" affair. Patterns were bought through mail order and made by seamstresses to the specifications of their wealthy patrons, whereas the masses either made garments themselves or bought them at retail venues. Clothing was a supreme communicator of one's rank in society, and sumptuary laws were frequently enacted to ensure that the lower classes could not assume false representation through fashion. Up to the Industrial Revolution and the advent of new manufacturing technology that surfaced shortly thereafter, fashion kept a status quo that was slow to change.

When Charles Frederick Worth set up shop in Paris during the late nineteenth century, he initiated the concept of an individual dictating fashion to the elite with seasonal offerings. Fashion was now a matter for the experts. By the turn of the century, however, views were changing and designers such as Poiret and Fortuny were challenging society's imposition of the corset, influenced by the suffragette movement. Their designs eliminated the corset and S-curve ideal, and enticed their audience with exotic Asian influences, as Europeans began to travel more. This liberation and increase in women's independence (a literal one, because women could now dress without the assistance of servants) created silhouettes that were easier to move about in and led to the surge of interest in recreation and sports.

Art, Design, and Youth

The onset of World War I led to fashion's focus on youth culture and the further reposition of women in society, many of whom cut their hair short, flattened their

◁ **Star quality** A star of the silver screen in the 20s and 30s, Greta Garbo brought fashion, glamour, and fantasy to the masses, particularly during the Depression era.

▽ **Youthful future** The advent of youth culture in the mid-twentieth century has served as the driving force for today's fashion designers. Fabric technology, synthetic dyes, and youthful proportions all underscore the intended audience for this collection.

chests, and adopted an androgynous "garçon" silhouette. The populace wanted to distance themselves from the harsh war years, and fashion became frivolous and fun, as did lifestyles that centered on parties, dancing the Charleston, and bootlegging. Coco Chanel was a catalyst for much of this, employing the fabric wool jersey that had traditionally been used only for men's undergarments. It was easy to move in, effortless to travel with, and accentuated the garçon figure. The forces of the art and design worlds also influenced fashion tremendously in an innovative synthesis, with cubist and art-deco motifs being employed through color and motif.

During the post-Depression 1940s, society sought a retreat from hardship, and Hollywood offered just that. Movie stars and the media created legends, and the designers who dressed them went for maximum impact and high glamour. Image was so important that film studios hired designers to dress their stars both on and off screen. Accessibility to the new "talkies," and star power, led to women trying to emulate their favorite silver-screen idols, such as Greta Garbo, Marlene Dietrich, and Joan Crawford. Vionnet's highly innovative bias-cut gowns conveyed glamour and left behind the more frivolous attitude of the 1920s, and Schiaparelli's humorous and surreal creations, influenced by Salvador Dalí and other surrealist artists, would remain the hallmarks of the era.

Rushing Forward

World War II rations restricted both fabric usage and availability, which created a raised hemline and slender silhouettes. Claire McCardell capitalized on the idea of separates to increase the looks within a wardrobe, and used denim, jersey, and lightweight cottons in simple shapes to be both stylish and practical. However, in the 1950s, fashion reacted against practicality and imposed restrictions. Women yearned for a new romantic silhouette, and Dior's swishing, voluminous skirts using up to 25 yards (23 m) of fabric defined the attitude.

The 1960s saw a pronounced youth culture that began defining the generation for itself. Designers were now catering to the young, who weren't dressing like their parents, but creating new ideas informed by pop culture and media events. Conveying status became less important, and the instigators of style responded to a more democratized society.

The following generations saw a speedier fashion world, and one that proposed new opportunities with every season, through an increased diversity of styles. Travel, technology, media, and new manufacturing techniques allowed designers to deliver their messages globally and at a much faster rate.

The diversity of design today has created an infinite quantity of fashion tribes that one can associate with. What does the future hold? With such speed of design, consumer awareness, and quantity of styles proposed, will trends and dictates be relevant anymore? What is the future of fashion design?

UNIT 3

designers
who define fashion history

The following pages feature a timeline of the key players in the fashion industry, from the late nineteenth century to the present day, including details on each designer's styles and key collections.

1910 1920 1930 1940 1950 1960 1970 1980 1990 2000

Charles Frederick Worth Latter half of the nineteenth century

Worth is largely known as the "father of couture." He revolutionized the practice of dressmaking by dictating trends and new looks to his wealthy clients, most notably Empress Josephine of France. Worth created the fashion show and the concept of in-house models.

Paul Poiret 1910s

Poiret popularized dresses that did not require a corset and exemplified the creative spirit of the burgeoning new century, particularly Orientalism. Poiret expanded his successful couture collections with new marketing ventures such as perfumes, cosmetics, accessories, and even interior-design products.

Mariano Fortuny 1910s

A true Renaissance man, Fortuny was a prolific artisan who dabbled in textiles, clothing, interior design, decorative arts, sculpture, painting, and more. His most notable contribution to fashion was the Greek-inspired, wrinkled silk dresses that were worn by actresses and wealthy women, along with exquisite, hand-painted, silk and velvet cocoon coats.

Jeanne Lanvin 1920s

Lanvin began her career in millinery, then shifted her business to childrenswear. She received such a positive response from women that she shifted again to focus primarily on womenswear, while retaining the youthful color palette and exuberance. The House of Lanvin is still open under the supervision of designer Alber Elbaz.

Paul Poiret fits a woman with one of his flamboyant creations. He made it his mission to make women's fashion bright, fun, and exotic.

Jean Patou 1920s

Apart from producing Joy, the world's most expensive perfume, Jean Patou was primarily known for developing sportswear for women that took advantage of the new importance of independence, physical activity, and health. The House of Patou has employed Karl Lagerfeld, Jean-Paul Gaultier, and Christian Lacroix, among other notable designers.

Madeleine Vionnet 1920s to 1930s

Vionnet contributed significantly to the technical aspects of dressmaking. Known for her work with the bias cut, Vionnet created dresses that took advantage of the new focus on physical health and slimness. She shifted the emphasis of construction away from pattern drafting to draping cloth on a figure, which allowed for graceful, fluid innovations.

Elsa Schiaparelli 1920s to 1930s

Without any formal training, Schiaparelli broke the rules to create fanciful and daring clothing and accessories. Schiaparelli created artistic fashion pieces of humor that appealed to a wide audience, and was inspired by her associations with artists Salvador Dalí, Christian Bérard, and Jean Cocteau. Her iconic high-heel-pump hat and the elegant gown that featured a large lobster painted on the side reflected the surrealist art movement.

1910 1920 1930

Gabrielle Chanel 1920s to 1960s

Gabrielle "Coco" Chanel shifted the prevailing aesthetic of the 1920s from ornate clothing to a sleek, unadorned, and modern look. After its success in the 1920s and 1930s, the House of Chanel was closed during World War II. In 1954, at the age of seventy, Chanel staged a comeback, reformulating her easy silhouettes for the needs of professional women in the 1950s and 1960s.

Cristóbal Balenciaga 1940s to 1950s

Balenciaga was a master of cut and precision, creating soft and elegant geometry on the body. He achieved a structured look without heavy boning by developing or using nontraditional fabrics such as silk gazar and silk ottoman. Spanish by birth, Balenciaga brought a romantic Spanish aesthetic to 1950s Paris, popularizing lace, the bolero, and red and black.

Hubert de Givenchy 1950s to 1960s

Givenchy's association with Audrey Hepburn often overshadows the talent and importance of this French designer. It just so happens that Givenchy created elegant and incredibly chic clothing for his famous muse. Givenchy was known for his clean, simple clothing that often featured whimsical trim or details.

Madame Grès 1930s

Alix Grès' first love was sculpture, which became evident in the sculpted gowns that she created. In 1936 she began using silk jersey, which had never been used in eveningwear before. Her travels to North Africa, Egypt, and India inspired beautiful gowns for her Western audience.

Christian Dior illustrates the new hemline from his 1953 collection, which gave women greater freedom of movement. The short skirt length caused a worldwide sensation.

Pierre Cardin 1950s to 1960s

Cardin is best known for his space-age work in the 1960s, and for his prodigious licencing agreements. Cardin was the first French couturier who broke with the Chambre Syndicale to design ready-to-wear and then a line of mens- and childrenswear, which many designers do today.

Claire McCardell 1940s to 1950s

McCardell was essential in the development of American sportswear as we know it today. During World War II, France was cut off from the rest of the world and American fashion designers had their first chance to exert their influence. McCardell developed easy-to-wear practical clothing that was based on mix-and-match separates. She is best known for the monastic dress, the popover dress, and the leotard.

Christian Dior Late 1940s to 1950s

In 1947, Dior introduced his groundbreaking Corolla collection to a war-weary Parisian audience. Overnight, the focus of fashion shifted to include wasp waists, slim shoulders, and full skirts that used yards of fabric. Dior continually defined feminine elegance season after season, introducing influential new looks during his relatively short career, which was ended by his untimely death in 1957.

Emilio Pucci 1950s to 1960s

An Italian nobleman by birth, Pucci was introduced to fashion by designing his own ski uniform. He introduced capri pants to the world in the 1950s as relaxed daywear for women. Pucci is best known for his unique and easily recognizable colorful silk prints featuring geometric and organic shapes.

Norman Norell 1940s to 1950s

Norell came into prominence during World War II when France was cut off from the United States. He developed clothing that established the American look with luxury fabrics in easy-to-wear silhouettes, and is particularly known for his sequin-covered "mermaid gowns." Norell's career spanned decades, making him a staple of the American fashion industry.

Charles James 1950s

James created eveningwear dresses that were feats of engineering and construction. Each ball gown perfectly shapes and sculpts the wearer, while remaining comfortable. Unfortunately, James' personality truncated his career and often precedes his dressmaking accomplishments.

Anne Klein 1950s to 1970s

A quintessential New York designer, Anne Klein had a long career creating easy, wearable mix-and-match clothing that answered young professional women's needs. She was the first designer to develop in-store boutiques, in which major department stores sectioned off part of the floor specifically for her merchandise, a standard practice today.

1910 1920 1930 1940 1950 1960 1970 1980 1990 2000

Yves Saint Laurent 1950s to 1980s

Few designers have been able to define the quixotic nature of the latter half of the twentieth century as well as Saint Laurent. Throughout his career he was able to characterize the changing attitudes of women and their position within society. From legitimizing pant suits for women in the 1960s to adapting utilitarian garments for high fashion and creating interest in ethnic diversity, Saint Laurent forged the way for others to follow.

Rudi Gernreich 1960s

Gernreich's early training as a modern dancer, and the sexual revolution of the 1960s, had a heavy influence on his design work. His clothing focused on an ease of movement and dramatic shapes, but emphasized open sexuality and freedom. Gernreich was also interested in communicating political and personal opinions on age, futurism, gender equality, and idealized beauty.

Valentino 1960s to early 2000s

For many women Valentino defined refined elegance in the latter half of the twentieth century. Actresses and socialites routinely wear his dramatic gowns to award shows or charity balls, often in his signature color of red.

Paco Rabanne 1960s

Rabanne's work was heavily influenced by architecture, the space age, and jewelry-making techniques. His work with linked metal chains and plastic disks is iconographic; his distinctive technique of using unique and unconventional materials has been influential for many designers.

Giorgio de Sant'Angelo 1960s to 1970s

Sant'Angelo was introduced to fashion through Diana Vreeland (*Vogue*'s influential fashion editor of the 1960s) after she saw his colorful jewelry. Sant'Angelo styled for *Vogue* in the early 1960s and opened his collection in 1966, creating distinctive looks that were influenced by the emphasis on ethnicity, exoticism, and the sexual revolution, featuring "Gypsy" looks and inspired by Native Americans.

Designers such as Ossie Clark continue to produce relevant and modern fashion for contemporary customers well past their formative years.

André Courrèges 1960s

Courrèges defined the era's fascination with all things space age for a whole generation by constructing clean, geometric, futuristic clothing. Both Mary Quant and Courrèges claim to have introduced the miniskirt, but each designer's aesthetic was unique. Courrèges' early training as an architect and his work for Balenciaga is seen in his strict color palettes and modern proportions.

Bonnie Cashin 1960s to 1970s

Cashin was a free-spirited but significant designer who created clothing for women with an active lifestyle. Primary hallmarks in her collections were layering, roomy but attractive shapes for ease of movement and comfort, and coordinated accessories for a complete look. She is also known for her toggle closures and leather binding on woolen fabrics.

Mary Quant 1960s

Quant is the designer most associated with the 1960s' emphasis on the young known as "youthquake." Understanding that young women of the post–World War II era did not want to look like their mothers, Quant introduced the miniskirt (along with André Courrèges in France), go-go boots, flat-heeled shoes, tights, and graphic prints, as well as popularizing the short Vidal Sassoon bowl haircut.

Ossie Clark 1960s to 1970s

Part of London's Chelsea scene, Clark created fun, whimsical clothing using printed fabrics in ornate, colorful patterns frequently designed by his wife. He was influenced by the bias-cut flowing dresses of the 1930s, and his interpretations set major trends. Clark designed for Mick Jagger and many of his female cohorts, along with several other popular rock stars of the time.

Sonia Rykiel 1960s to present

The "queen of knits" almost exclusively designs in knits, and provided comfortable but sexy pieces for women during the 1960s and '70s. Popularizing the shrunken poor-boy top and knit pants, Rykiel has become a stylish French icon of comfort and practicality.

Karl Lagerfeld 1960s to present

A prolific and intuitive designer, Karl Lagerfeld's influence is pervasive throughout the fashion industry. Lagerfeld's genius comes from a true postmodernist sense of the combinations and possibilities of style. He is best known for his association with the House of Chanel, updating and invigorating the label by combining trademark signatures of the House with street fashion and a youthful perspective.

Emanuel Ungaro 1970s to 1980s

Ungaro is best known for his treatment of prints, combining patterns and colors in an unexpected way. His clothing was always feminine and elegant, but also playful with its array of colors, textures, and prints.

Perry Ellis 1970s to 1980s

Starting out as a merchandiser allowed Ellis to closely observe the all-important marketing and retail components of fashion. Women were expanding their role in the workforce and Perry Ellis was an essential designer in the development of American classics, providing mix-and-match clothing that met their daily needs.

Halston 1970s

A major influence on American sportswear in the 1970s, Halston's clothing relied on simple, flattering construction that looked great on multiple body types. His pieces were generally monochromatic and made out of luxury fabrics with a long and lean silhouette. Halston used his associations with a wide variety of celebrities, as well as his visits to Studio 54, to cement his iconic, celebrity status.

Kenzo Takada 1970s to 1980s

One of the first Japanese designers to emigrate to Paris, Kenzo was an early example of a fresh perspective in 1970s French fashion. He is known for his playful silhouettes and original combinations of patterns, prints, and bold colors.

Mixing Asian and western influences through unique prints and fluid silhouettes, Kenzo was a star of 1970s Parisian fashion.

Missoni 1970s to 1980s

The unique patterns and colors of Missoni knits are unmistakable, affording the company easy recognition and popularity. The wearable and artful collections tapped into what women were looking for: clothes that were distinctive but functional in women's professional lives.

Stephen Burrows 1970s

Burrows is best known for his graphically colored and soft, clingy shapes made predominantly in silk chiffon and matte jersey. His dresses are often asymmetrical and feature a "lettuce edge" finishing detail at the hem.

Jean-Charles de Castelbajac
1970s to 1980s

Castelbajac became popular in the 1970s when he started to use ordinary or common materials such as sleeping bags, blankets, or teddy bears to create unique designs. His style was irreverently humorous, becoming more art-to-wear than ready-to-wear.

Bill Blass 1970s to 1980s

A classic American designer, Bill Blass helped to define the American look of sleek sophistication and elegant grace. Blass developed several different clothing lines and licencing agreements to meet the needs of a variety of women in any aspect of their lives.

Geoffrey Beene 1970s to 1980s

Beene was an innovator and rebel within the American fashion industry. As a former medical student, Beene always focused on the three-dimensional qualities of form and how shape rotates around the female body. Beene's work is often characterized by his use of nontraditional fabrics that create geometric forms, the triangle as motif, and positive/negative shape to reveal areas of the body.

James Galanos 1970s to 1980s

Galanos was an American couturier in craftsmanship, detail, and price. Creating gowns for a rarefied few, he became more widely known when Nancy Reagan chose his gowns for presidential functions in the 1980s.

1970

1920 1930 1940 1950 1960 1970 1980 1990 2000

Issey Miyake 1970s to 1990s

Miyake has combined art and fashion in clothes that are effortlessly wearable and attractive. Miyake's work combines his interest in sculptural form with Eastern and Western aesthetics and innovative experiments with fabric. Miyake is best known for his work with architectural pleating systems under the Pleats Please and APOC (A Piece Of Cloth) lines.

Vivienne Westwood 1970s to present

Throughout Westwood's lengthy career she has been inspired by pop culture, historicism, and the strong independent woman she designs for. She began her career in the 1970s with a store, then opened her own label. Employing themes such as romantic pirates, eighteenth- and nineteenth-century aristocrats, and eco-warriors, she never abandons her focus on confident, sexy women.

Thierry Mugler 1980s

Drawing from the postmodern and underground cultures of sexual fetishes, nightclubs, science fiction, and pin-up Hollywood, Mugler created a theatrical style that was influenced by his background in dance. Mugler produced an aggressive, highly tailored look for confident women with armor shapes, exaggerated shoulders, padded hips, and wasp waists.

Calvin Klein 1970s to 1990s

An astute businessman and marketer, Klein propelled the New York fashion industry forward by considering advertising and multiple markets in a whole new way. Klein used controversial advertising, featuring varying degrees of nudity and raw sexuality. His clothing was rich with traditional American classics, elevated by glamorous and mysterious marketing campaigns.

Claude Montana 1980s to early 1990s

Montana was an integral designer of the 1980s and early 1990s, creating highly architectural pieces with large shoulders, heavy metal studs and embellishments, and short tight skirts. Montana's woman was strong, powerful, and intimidating, an image which many women were looking for as they forged new pathways into upper-level professional jobs.

Oscar de la Renta 1970s to present

Oscar de la Renta is known for his romantic, often ruffled eveningwear, which is sometimes inspired by his upbringing in the Dominican Republic and his studies in Spain and Paris. He was the first American to have the distinct honor of showing his collections in Paris.

Vivienne Westwood celebrates history by using period fashion for inspirations in her grand, romantic work.

Azzedine Alaïa 1980s to 1990s

Alaïa has created a sexy, body-conscious style that is easily recognized and synonymous with female strength. He helped to define the look of the 1980s by relying on toned, muscular female celebrities such as Tina Turner, Raquel Welch, and Grace Jones to best express his constructed knit dresses.

Giorgio Armani 1970s to present

Armani started out as a menswear designer in 1974 and opened his womenswear collection the next year. Always known for his soft tailoring, an Armani suit in the 1980s became ubiquitous with power dressing. The suit remains central to his business, along with his associations with Hollywood movie stars, both male and female, on the red carpet.

Stephen Sprouse 1980s

A major figure in the New York City downtown scene, Sprouse often used elements of pop culture such as 1960s, '70s, and '80s music culture, graffiti, and the artwork of Andy Warhol, Keith Haring, and Basquiat. He is well known for his use of neon colors with black, along with his unique handwriting used for prints.

Gianni Versace 1980s to early 1990s

Versace was known for his bright, flashy clothing that exuded a rock 'n' roll attitude while using beautiful silks, leathers, and knits. He used Greek, Roman, and art-deco motifs in brightly colored prints, alongside the fashion house's emblem, the head of Medusa. Versace was also well known for his close associations with celebrities, including Elton John and Elizabeth Hurley.

Romeo Gigli 1980s to early 1990s

Romeo Gigli eschewed the trappings of current glamorous fashion to create his own ideal and focused vision. Gigli routinely relied on rich jewel-tone colors and sensual fabrics that harkened back to the Renaissance and Byzantine eras, while being preeminently modern in his romantic silhouettes and iconic cocoon coats.

Yohji Yamamoto 1980s to present

Yamamoto often uses black fabric that does not conform to a body shape, symmetry, or fashion trends. Preferring to express alternatives to traditional notions of sex appeal, Yamamoto strives to create beauty and spirituality through dramatic silhouette. He is well known for his collaboration with Adidas under the Y3 label.

Marc Jacobs 1980s to present

Marc Jacobs is arguably the most well-known and influential American designer today. Jacobs created great notoriety in his early career as the creator of the infamous Grunge collection for Perry Ellis, inspired by the Seattle-based, post-punk music scene of the 1990s. He has since become increasingly popular as the designer of his eponymous lines as well as being the design director for Louis Vuitton in Paris.

Ralph Lauren 1980s to present

Ralph Lauren is considered by many to be a marketing genius because he has developed a well-honed brand identity that focuses on traditional icons of aspiration. Lauren came into prominence in the 1980s, allowing people to adopt the Ivy League look. He continued to use American signatures and inspirations derived from Native American culture, the Wild West, and early Hollywood, all with great commercial success.

Donna Karan 1980s to present

Karan created a significant shift in the way working women of the 1980s thought about dressing. An executive herself, Karan created a professional wardrobe that focused on essentials and allowed for full movement and comfort, while not being restricted to the masculine suits that were currently offered. She is also a proponent of organically draped, sensual dresses that contrast with her more tailored sportswear.

Prada uses complex concepts and theories to question where fashion's future will be directed.

Jean-Paul Gaultier 1980s to present

Gaultier's enduring contribution to fashion is his examination of gender roles and use of different cultural and religious groups as forms of inspiration. Gaultier has helped women feel strong and powerful yet sexy, while also creating menswear that exemplifies a more feminine sense of beauty and sensuality.

Martine Sitbon 1980s to present

Sitbon came into prominence in the 1980s with her work for Chloé, under her own label in the 1990s, and in the millennium with Byblos. She combines soft structure based on menswear elements with a sensitive color palette and music-culture inspirations.

Rei Kawakubo 1980s to present

Designing under the label Comme des Garçons, Kawakubo is the "philosopher of fashion" and one of the chief advocates of the deconstruction aesthetic introduced in the late 1970s. She creates clothing with a deeper commentary on image, the body, and sex appeal, and consistently challenges silhouette, fabric, and presentation.

Christian Lacroix 1980s to present

Lacroix has been a symbol of couture extravagance his entire career. First introduced as the designer for the House of Patou, Lacroix gained popularity for his iconic pouf skirt dress that was a favorite during the extravagant 1980s. Lacroix continues to fascinate with bright color palettes and ornate fabrics, often executed in a highly decorative manner.

Prada 1990s to present

Miuccia Prada has successfully shifted the focus of the venerable Italian luxury leather company, founded by her grandfather, to a leading name in the world of fashion. Creating fashion that often pushes the notion of what is ugly and elegant, Prada consistently aims to create clothing that women cannot be defined by. She has stated that she purposely uses fabric or concepts that she hates for the challenge it creates.

1990

| | 1910 | 1920 | 1930 | 1940 | 1950 | 1960 | 1970 | 1980 | 1990 | 2000 |

Gucci/Tom Ford 1990s to early 2000s

Originally an Italian luxury leather goods company, Gucci was quietly producing fashion until Tom Ford joined the company in the 1990s. By 1995, Gucci and Tom Ford were receiving premier press amplified by a steady celebrity and socialite following. Tom Ford combined assertive silhouettes reminiscent of the 1970s with a contemporary, sexy twist.

Martin Margiela 1990s to present

Highly influential in contemporary fashion, Margiela was a member of the original Antwerp Six. He has always treated fashion as a philosophical pursuit, working from cerebral concepts such as deconstructionism and unconventional perceptions of beauty. He ignores trends, preferring to rework existing ideas until they are exhausted in his own artistic process.

Dries Van Noten 1990s to present

Originally part of the Antwerp Six collective, Van Noten has established himself as a very different designer from the other five designers originally from Belgium. Van Noten's work is often marked by an eclectic combination of silhouettes, colors, and prints inspired by places such as India, Central Asia, and, of course, Europe.

Jil Sander 1990s to early 2000s

Jil Sander was a leader of the minimalist movement begun in the 1990s, preferring to work in largely monochromatic color palettes with as little seaming and details as possible. Popularizing the unlined, soft-shoulder jacket, she fitted in perfectly with the 1990s, a time when women were interested in quiet materialism after the flamboyant '80s.

Dolce & Gabbana 1990s to present

The Italian designers Domenico Dolce and Stefano Gabbana frequently use Italian iconography, sex, and controversial advertising to promote their label. Originally referencing Sicilian heritage, their collections have evolved and often use leopard print, corsets, and the colors black and red to produce form-fitting, sexy clothing.

Ann Demeulemeester 1990s to present

A member of the Antwerp Six, Demeulemeester works within a strict color palette most often focused on the color black. Her clothing is a play on opposites, namely the slouchy menswear-inspired lines contrasted with a romanticism and softness that appears in every collection. She often cites singer Patti Smith as an inspiration and muse for her work.

Helmut Lang 1990s to early 2000s

A leader of the minimalist movement in the 1990s, Lang's work was reliant on a graphic and monochromatic color palette along with high-tech fabrics. Lang often used bold geometric shapes, stiff silhouettes, utilitarian details, and sheer fabrics to create a graphic and military quality for both his men's and women's androgynous clothing.

Isaac Mizrahi 1990s to present

Mizrahi is consistently inspired by two types of women: the Hollywood actress of the 1950s and the savvy New York woman. His clothing is bright and cheerful but never childish, often relying on familiar, simple silhouettes that employ unique texture and color combinations. Mizrahi has become a widely recognized designer because of his documentary movie *Unzipped* and his charismatic personality.

John Galliano 1990s to present

Galliano is known for his historical odes to dress as much as for his grand runway productions that require enormous sums of money to produce and always create a press sensation. Producing under his own label as well as for the House of Dior, Galliano's work is focused on highly glamorous, historically referenced, and exquisitely crafted gowns that have made him notorious in the world of contemporary fashion.

Paul Smith 1990s to present

Smith started out as a menswear designer, creating clothing for men who were interested in breaking free of the traditional three-piece suit but still needed to appear professional. Smith uses bright, bold colors alongside classic silhouettes. In 1998 he opened a womenswear collection and operates retail stores around the world.

Michael Kors 1990s to present

Kors has developed a loyal following for his playful, relaxed approach to American classics. Creating wearable and comfortable clothing with a lighthearted twist, often rooted in uniquely American themes such as Palm Beach and Aspen, Kors uses bold graphic patterns and colors along with sportswear staples of camel, charcoal, black, and white.

Alberta Ferretti 1990s to present

Ferretti is often inspired by her Italian roots when producing her richly colored cocktail dresses. Known for the dressmaker details in her feminine dresses, Ferretti has a loyal following of jet-set elite.

1990

Alexander McQueen 1990s to present

McQueen has always been controversial, and is consistently watched by anyone associated with fashion. He combines a rebellious view of fashion and beauty with incredible tailoring skills that he picked up from his apprenticeships on Savile Row in London. McQueen couples these with the eye of a showman and fashion historian, creating runway performance pieces that continue to shift the future of fashion.

Alexander McQueen juxtaposes period references with modern fabrics and techniques.

Stella McCartney Early 2000s

The daughter of the former Beatle Sir Paul McCartney achieved her own fame after becoming the design director for the House of Chloé. In 2001 she joined the Gucci Group to form her eponymous line. She is known as much for her outspoken views on animal rights as she is for her own brand of updated 1970s and '80s classics, unique prints, and interesting tailored pieces that are geared to a youthful consumer.

Narciso Rodriguez Early 2000s

Rodriguez came to international prominence after creating the simple yet elegant wedding dress for Carolyn Bessette Kennedy to John F. Kennedy Jr. His training at Calvin Klein influenced his own sense of minimalist style, which uses a graphic color palette with precise seaming and construction details. He brings a fresh perspective to wearable clothing.

Proenza Schouler Early 2000s

Despite their youth, the designers Lazaro Hernandez and Jack McCoullough have proven themselves to be a design team with lasting power. The creative duo approaches style and culture through a fresh perspective that has earned them numerous prestigious accolades within the fashion world.

Hussein Chalayan Early 2000s

Chalayan is an artist, philosopher, and designer of innovative, wearable clothing. Ignoring trends, Chalayan creates clothing, runway-show theatrics, and music that seamlessly blend into each other to shape a performance piece of abstract meaning. As a conceptual designer, he is consistently cited in books as an example of a designer who is more interested in the mind than the pocketbook.

Junya Watanabe Early 2000s

A protégé of Rei Kawakubo of Comme des Garçons, Watanabe is known for his remarkable construction techniques and his adoption of technologically advanced fabrics. He frequently chooses one theme for his collection, often deconstructing and reconstructing a singular idea in an amazing array of versions.

Veronique Branquinho Early 2000s

Veronique Branquinho is known for her subtle, muted colors and clever mixing of masculine construction with soft, feminine drape and texture.

Francisco Costa Early 2000s

Costa, known for his spare, graphic, and experimental style, has shifted the image of the House of Calvin Klein. He has used a variety of colors, from acidic layers of citrus to pearly whites and deep blacks, while maintaining the architectural aesthetic developed by founder Klein. Costa frequently innovates silhouette and develops many of the futuristic fabrics and prints that are exclusive to the House.

Nicolas Ghesquière Early 2000s

Ghesquière is often described as a futurist, experimenting with shape, color, fabrics, and construction, to create consistently trendsetting pieces. Since 1997, at the age of twenty-six, Ghesquière has worked under the House of Balenciaga, closely examining the master's collections and interpreting the ideals of the House in a wholly unique and futuristic way.

Viktor & Rolf Early 2000s

Dutch designers Viktor Horsting and Rolf Snoeren repeatedly challenge the fashion status quo and create shows that explore innovative fabrics, silhouette, and wearability. Their surrealist and abstracted approach to fashion has made them the subject of several books, along with gallery and museum shows that highlight the connections between art and fashion.

UNIT 4
primary categories in the market

Fashion design is grouped by categories to suggest price point, aesthetic, and the targeted audience. It is vital that you understand the category you are designing for.

Haute Couture

Haute couture is the most expensive, well-made, and labor-intensive type of clothing, and it is strictly monitored by the Chambre Syndicale de la Haute Couture in Paris. To be a couturier, a designer must be invited by the Chambre Syndicale, practice in Paris, and employ at least fifteen workers. A fashion show of at least thirty-five pieces in both evening- and daywear must be presented twice yearly. Garments must be specifically fit to each customer at least three times.

Couture began with Charles Frederick Worth in the latter half of the nineteenth century, but has declined in popularity because of the exorbitant costs and exhaustive process. Designers use couture primarily as a way to garner attention for their prêt-á-porter collections.

Designer/Prêt-á-Porter

This category describes collections that use standardized sizing and hold seasonal showings for the fashion press and buyers. Designer-level clothing is marked by superior fabrics, construction, and workmanship, and often has a cachet attached to the collections either by extensive marketing and advertising—such as Donna Karan—or by attention to construction and detail—such as Hermès. Designer-level clothing can also be known for more esoteric, conceptual, and abstract inspirations that explore artistic and philosophical ideas, as with the work of Comme des Garçons and Hussein Chalayan.

Increasingly, designer/prêt-á-porter collections are becoming rarefied and used as a promotional tool for fashion houses to sell their less expensive licences and diffusion collections.

△ **Classic couture techniques**
There is rarely a price limit on couture because of its emphasis on quality and techniques that must be done by hand. The labor, skill, and vast amount of time required make this skirt with hand-applied, picot-edged, bias-cut, silk strips couture.

Bridge

This market originally gained prominence in the 1970s when women were entering the workforce en masse, and were unable to find suitable clothing that answered their professional needs. Bridge is more of an American phenomenon, relying on the classic American looks of sportswear and business suits for women. Bridge can be of a higher price point, though not as high as designer lines because there is not the same designer name cachet, and less superior fabrics and manufacturing processes are employed.

The style and silhouettes of the bridge market did not change much from season to season. Since women were entering the workforce and sensitive to being perceived by their male coworkers as too feminine, designers responded by using traditional male suiting colors such as gray, black, navy, and taupe in their tailored clothing for women. In the 1980s designers began offering women alternative silhouettes that allowed them to feel professional while not ignoring their feminine side.

Today's bridge market is in a state of flux because baby-boomer women feel more comfortable competing with men in the workforce, and younger women do not necessarily feel pressured to—or want to—wear suits. Therefore, many bridge collections, such as Banana Republic or Anne Taylor, are less expensive and more stylistically adventurous to appeal to the younger female customer.

◁ **Silhouette innovation**
Designer-level collections use top-quality fabrics for highly original designs. The sculptural forms and fabric technology employed in this collection demonstrates an innovative point of view.

▽ **Familiar silhouettes**
By addressing familiar silhouettes with high-quality fabrics, practicality, and a well-balanced color palette, Bridge collections offer consumers a complete wardrobe of mix-and-match separates that contain well-conceived details.

Contemporary

The contemporary market is equal in price point to bridge, but is for a younger and more adventurous customer. Many designers have diffusion lines, such as Donna Karan's DKNY, Calvin Klein's CK, Dolce & Gabbana's D&G, that would be included in this category. These customers pay attention to larger fashion trends and what designers put on the runway, but want fashion at a lower price point.

Moderate

Moderate clothing collections are sold in department stores such as Macy's, Dillard's, or JCPenney, which serve customers in a variety of activities from business attire to weekend wear. Also in this category are labels that are more active or casual and found in shopping centers, such as Gap, Abercrombie & Fitch, and The Limited. Silhouettes are interpreted from selected designers' collections or are based on the preceding year's sales.

Clothing is divided into core, core plus, and novelty items. A core piece is one that everyone wears and is in traditional colors; for example, jeans in Gap, a navy skirt in Macy's. A core plus item is a standard silhouette with a twist; for example, a striped sweater or a navy skirt with ruffles at the hem. A novelty item is trendy in silhouette and color, and adds excitement.

Tweens/Juniors

Tweens are children from the ages of ten to fourteen, and juniors are teenagers from thirteen to eighteen. These markets have expanded exponentially within the twenty-first century because both baby boomers and Generation X members have children who like to shop. As children are encouraged to create their unique identities by their parents, marketers seize upon the opportunity to sell more products. As soon as a trend is widely accepted, it is considered passé. Labels in this category include Forever 21, Delia's, and Old Navy.

Budget

Budget is by far the fastest-growing segment of the fashion industry. Within every customer category there will be a budget alternative as consumers demand lower-cost merchandise. High-concept and high-price designers from Stella McCartney, Karl Lagerfeld, and Rei Kawakubo have created collections for the Swedish retailer H&M. Isaac Mizrahi created his own label for Target, and Proenza Schouler, Alexander McQueen, Jonathan Saunders, Tracy Reese, and others have created collections under the Go International label for Target.

The budget market requires that retailers produce clothing inexpensively and quickly. This brings new meaning to the term "seasonal dressing," because inexpensive fabrics and trendy silhouettes last for only a short time. Growing attention is being paid to the unfair and dangerous labor practices of clothing manufacturers that exploit workers to try to meet the price limitations of retailers. Harsh criticism has also been centered on the clothing industry for creating so much "throwaway" clothing that gets dumped in landfills, and for creating cheap fabrics that are harmful to the environment.

▷▷ **Utilitarian updates** Casual silhouettes, fabrics such as cotton denim and twill, attention to design details, and youthful colors give a casual feel to this tweens/juniors grouping. The price point must ensure the fabrics and production costs remain within limits, and designs appeal to a youthful, active audience.

▷ **Screen tests** This contemporary brand uses suggestive imagery to appeal to a youthful audience. Brands targeting youth culture frequently hire celebrities for campaigns to benefit from their large fan base and strong image.

UNIT 5
seasonal deliveries

The six basic seasons most designers create collections for are transition, fall, holiday, resort/pre-spring, spring, and summer.

Fall and spring are the primary seasons with the largest collections, whereas the others are smaller "capsule" collections.

High-priced collections have fewer deliveries because the clothing is more labor intensive and expensive to produce. Lower-priced collections—such as budget—may have new deliveries every other week to entice customers. Many stores will keep multiple deliveries on the floor; as such, designers must be sensitive to how fabrics and colors flow from one delivery into the next, so items may work together.

△ **Fall forest**
Brown, ochre, ivory, and maroon give a sense of comfort and warmth to cold-weather fabrics in a fall/winter collection. Dark colors also wear well in the seasonal elements.

TRANSITION

- This is a small collection aimed at enticing the customer to get excited about fall. Traditional colors that remind the customer of the season include: browns, pumpkin, olive green, cranberry, aubergine, rust, and ochre.

FALL *In stores for September*

- Traditional colors are gray, black, and taupe, along with any "trending" colors.
- Fabrics are textural and heavy to suit the weather.

HOLIDAY *In stores by November*

- A smaller capsule collection.
- Traditional colors are black, metallics, champagne, and jewel tones.
- Fabrics are usually dressy and aimed at the special occasion, such as velvets, lace, and satins.
- Gift-giving knits are also important in this season and use specialty yarns such as angora, chenille, and cashmere.

RESORT/PRE-SPRING *In stores by December/January*

- Small capsule collection, often a tease for the spring collection.
- Colors are bright and pastel, intended to attract consumers dealing with winter doldrums.
- Swimsuits and spring clothing are often introduced at this point for those who are taking a vacation to a warmer climate.

SPRING *In stores by February*

- A larger collection that may have several deliveries. Emphasis is on layering for ease of adjustment to changing temperatures.
- Silhouettes are transitional with fabrics of cottons, silk knits, and generally lighter fabrics and colors.

SUMMER *In stores by April/May*

- Bright colors, fabrics, and prints.
- Silhouettes are generally more casual and relaxed, and less layered.

△ **Watercolor hothouse florals** Spring/summer collections often use colors that are primary and saturated. The dominance of white and floral-inspired colors relates to the warm season through references to nature.

UNIT 6
customer profiles: lifestyle

All designers work with a specific customer in mind. Defining your customer keeps you focused and your collections cohesive.

By creating a narrative around your customer, you will begin to develop a clear personality that you can refer to when selecting fabrics, colors, and prints. This customer sketch can also inform your choices in silhouette development, merchandising, and even the usage of your designs: What some customers consider eveningwear others may consider daywear.

Profile A:
The Successful Gallery Owner

A married woman, thirty-five years old, works in an art gallery selling successful contemporary artists such as Elizabeth Peyton, Dana Schultz, and Ryan McGinley. She earns a high salary and lives in a newly renovated, low-rise loft building in Chelsea in New York City, with her husband, a VP in finance. She favors independent films shown at the Film Forum, and frequently attends modern dance performances choreographed by Mark Morris and Martha Graham. She travels to learn about culture rather than rest at a spa or beach resort. She is always looking for what's innovative in the design world, and her frequent travels around the world to search for new artists in urban capitals allow her to see global cutting-edge design. Much of her wardrobe is dedicated to looking professional at work, but with a highly individual flair. She enjoys wearing Yohji Yamomoto, Commes des Garçons, and Rick Owens because of their unorthodox construction techniques and sculptural silhouettes.

Lifestyle Questions

When creating your customer profile, consider the following questions as a framework.

THE BASICS:

Age?

Occupation? Level of job?

Residency? Be specific. If New York City, do they live in the Upper East Side, East Village, Meat Packing District, etc? Urban neighborhoods often have a particular feel and population.

Single or married? Children?

Education level? University attended? Course of study?

PREFERENCES:

Favorite movies?

Types of vacation favored? Locations favored?

Favorite restaurants?

Magazines subscribed to?

Favorite artists and/or art movements?

Favorite music? Bands?

Other designers favored?

By answering these questions it is easy to see how a fairly thorough insight into a person can keep your collections focused.

▷ **Silhouette sculptures** The effort and confidence required to wear dramatic silhouettes contribute to defining a very particular customer. Bold, linear patterns juxtapose with the organic forms to emphasize the collection's confident personality.

◁ **Knitted confections** Fine-gauge and intricately patterned knitwear in neutral tones conveys a soft and feminine feel. The complex stitches maintain the design focus because of the familiar and easy-to-wear garment silhouettes.

Profile B:
The Student and Teen Vogue Intern

A single girl, twenty-one years old, who interns at *Teen Vogue* in New York City. She is a journalism student at Columbia University and doesn't have much disposable income for her wardrobe, but she is aware of fashion and has a lot of fun styling herself. She's young and feminine at heart, loves romantic comedies and any movie starring Kate Winslet, and envies her mother's wardrobe, which includes such historical greats as Ossie Clark and Halston. When she's not at work, she's often at the local coffee shop with friends, listening to the latest underground bands perform.

Her style is all-American, so practicality and comfort are most important to her. Her favorite labels are Marc by Marc Jacobs and A.P.C., both of which tend to have slim fits, classic fabrics and colors, and will still be considered "in trend" for seasons to come.

▽ **Not a wallflower** Whimsical texture combinations, neon colors, and attention-grabbing detail convey a youthful customer who prefers form that functions. Novelty fabrics and proportions suggest a mood, time, and place for wear.

UNIT 7
analysis of advertisements

What makes you stay loyal to one particular brand? Why do we aspire to be part of one fashion group and not another? What makes you prefer a simple black suit from one designer over the others?

Designers use advertising as the most accessible method for displaying and articulating their "tribe" to consumers in the hope that they will want to be a part of their fictitious world. Fashion is frequently about association. The clothing we choose to wear denotes a particular lifestyle we are part of (or wish to join) because it is the first impression that we make before verbal exchanges are made. Fashion is nonverbal communication.

By acquiring the basic skills for analyzing advertisements, you will become more sensitive to your customer's development and how it can be accentuated. Learning how advertisers and art directors use the model, styling, lighting, choice of props, setting, and other hallmarks will give you the tools not only to acquire a versatility of design, but also help you view design as problem solving.

It is important to remember that when defining your customer, some of your choices for communicating your vision will be defined by your intended audience. Some customers need lots of information to describe the "world" proposed by the designer, whereas other customers may appreciate something more abstract and artistic.

CONSIDER THE FOLLOWING WHEN ANALYZING FASHION ADS:

What is the setting/location?

How does the environment enhance the message?

What props are used? What do they communicate?

Consider the model's age, pose, and attitude.

Think about the lighting and its positioning. How does it elevate the mood?

In what position is the viewer/camera?

Take into account the time of day and time of year. Are they specific or generic? Why?

Is a narrative conveyed? How does this reflect upon the targeted customer?

What other models or "characters" are in the photo and what is their relevance? Do they add to the narrative? How?

Consider the composition of the ad and how it reflects on the targeted audience.

What publication is the ad in? Whom does it speak to?

Invigorating a Brand

The effectiveness of this Burberry advertisement is partly because of how it relates to the viewer, through setting, scale, and placement. The outdoor street scene works seamlessly with the viewers' urban environment and allows them to be part of the advertisement experience. The model's life-size proportion enhances the viewer's participation, as she appears to be on the street with her audience.

Black and white photography suggests classicism and heritage, like a favorite classic film, while the model's age, pose, and foreground composition convey a youthful and confident customer. The iconic automobile imparts its status and prestige onto the Burberry brand through association. By posing the model with the Rolls Royce to suggest ownership, wealth is conveyed and suggests that the well-heeled and fashionable choose Burberry. The iconic Burberry plaid is given maximum exposure through umbrella lining, scarf, and perfume bottle, much the same as a logo may communicate a brand.

The A-line silhouette made by the model's pose and the diagonal line of the car's placement moves the viewer's eye to prevent stagnation; this reinforces the energetic, youthful feel for the customer and brand's identity.

Chasing the Dream

The casual attitude of Dolce and Gabbana's diffusion line D&G is well portrayed in this ad that underscores its denim focus. Bringing to mind the paintings of Paul Cadmus and other artists who worked during and post–World War II, the advertisement romanticizes the military lifestyle through highly stylized models and a staged composition.

The denim category is emphasized through indigo tones and a naval setting to suggest utilitarian workwear. The addition of red accents completes the patriotic color combination of red, "white," and blue.

The models are of similar age and seem to represent a more idealized masculinity and personification of the military lifestyle. This is conveyed by the seemingly lackadaisical attitude of the models aboard the warship as they lounge around reading and daydreaming despite the pressures of military service. The lack of an active and performance narrative allows the viewers to focus on the fashions rather than a thematic aspect, which could divert their attention and overshadow the product being marketed.

The circular composition keeps the viewers' eyes roaming so they are sure to appreciate and study all of the garment details and shapes. Viewers are invited to be a part of this romance through setting, mood, and idealization, so they may buy into the collection, no matter how unrelated the garments may be to naval paraphernalia.

design foundations

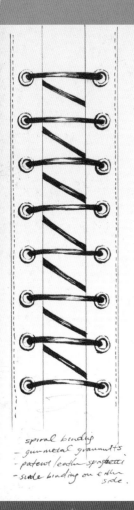

spiral binding
- gunmetal grummetts
- patent leather spaghetti
- suade binding on either side.

Acquiring a solid foundation of quantitative and qualitative research is core to producing successful and prolific design. How you research and use this material is your choice, but it often comes down to experimentation and exposing yourself to anything and everything in your early development so that you learn what stimulates your creativity most. Whether it's street culture, museums and galleries, architecture, historical costume, technology, unfamiliar cultures, or narratives found in literature and film, there is always a concept waiting to be researched and applied to fashion design.

This chapter explores many of the primary "umbrellas" that designers research to create fashion, and how each area may contribute to developing a unique vision. Designing with color, motif, fabric textures, fabric weights, and silhouette are skills that must be mastered when developing a collection to accentuate a mood, merchandise successfully, maintain design cohesion, and keep a saturated point of view.

· collection palette ·

· traditional chic palette ·

△▷ **Attention to detail**
Designers consider every small detail, which must support the collection's aesthetic.

▷ **Color categories**
Palettes underscore an inspiration, customer aesthetic, season, and design category.

· lounge / casual palette ·

◁ **Design cohesion** Beginning with well-edited research and a defined motif ensures a focused collection. Accent colors are used in varying proportions, treatments, and placements to bring this collection development together.

◺▷ **Silhouette definition** These simple, vertical silhouettes focus the design on the complex pattern and scale relationships.

UNIT 8
research

Inspiration can be found through planned research or serendipitously. Collating research and presenting it in an inspiration book will prove indispensable when it comes to generating fresh ideas.

Primary Research

Primary research is original material that is collected and synthesized by the designer. It might be collected from seeing original artwork, artifacts in a museum, or sketching historical garments. Designers also might look at historical pictures, furniture design, or scientific images of plants and animals to gather information about details, ideas, forms, colors, or textures. All the information is gathered to feed your own imagination and design process.

▷ **Cultural hub**
An established museum or gallery, such as the V&A, London, is a rich resource for research and inspiration. The building itself can be inspiring, along with the varied contents.

Secondary Research

Secondary research is information that has been accumulated and synthesized for the designer. It may be through trend forecasting provided by a service or a fashion magazine, in which there are several examples of other designers using a focused area of information and inspiration. Interpretations of important colors, fabrics, textures, and style details may be highlighted from several designers to show a common idea.

▷ **Creative license** A mind map allows designers to see how an inspiration can relate to other contexts for deeper relationships. Word association and stream-of-consciousness writing are all you need to discover what types of additional research can be investigated and applied.

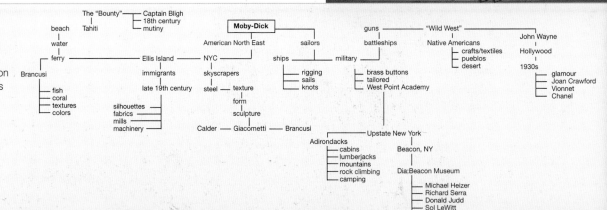

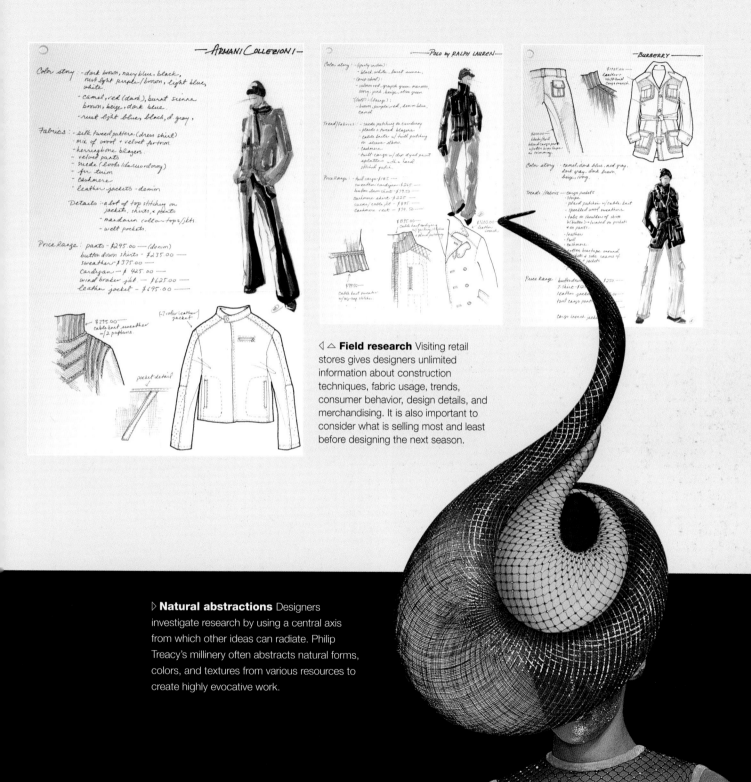

Field research Visiting retail stores gives designers unlimited information about construction techniques, fabric usage, trends, consumer behavior, design details, and merchandising. It is also important to consider what is selling most and least before designing the next season.

▷ **Natural abstractions** Designers investigate research by using a central axis from which other ideas can radiate. Philip Treacy's millinery often abstracts natural forms, colors, and textures from various resources to create highly evocative work.

▽ **Everything's coming up roses** In the complex layered sleeve detail of an Alexander McQueen creation, an intricately constructed silk bodice echoes the tightly furled petals of a rosebud. (Fall/Winter 2008, Paris Fashion Week)

Inspiration Books: The World at Large

As a designer, creating a visual "diary" is beneficial for many reasons. It enables you to store inspirational material in one location so that you may reference it efficiently, and collecting well-edited material may spawn other types of ideas for research and design (see the mind map on pages 32–33). It will also allow you to reflect on your natural instincts as a designer over time and indicate where you are heading creatively.

Anything can be a source of inspiration for fashion design, and this is exactly how you should approach the task of adding researched material to your book. Images of artwork, architecture, furniture and interior design, photographs taken on vacation, fabric swatches, wallpaper samples, pieces of creative writing, spontaneous sketches done in a café, color references from magazines or paint chips from the hardware store, photos of garment details, images of beading and embroidery techniques, textures, and even a model's attitude can all contribute to a rich source of material to work from. If you see something that elicits a strong creative reaction, store it in your book.

Your inspiration book should always be thought of as a place to store raw, unrefined material that you can then extract and use to develop more fleshed-out, well-researched, and clearly articulated themes that you will then design from.

Store images loosely before mounting them into your book. This will allow you to group images into similar themes and ideas for better visual articulation.

CONSIDER THE FOLLOWING WHEN DEVELOPING YOUR BOOK:

- How can I make my research rich and diverse?
- What sources will give me broad types of research?
- How can page layout and composition accentuate my design aesthetic?
- Is my research clearly communicating my message to an unfamiliar viewer?
- Is the material generating my creativity sufficiently?
- How can I make the research more focused by adding/editing?
- Does the research generated lead to new areas for exploration?
- Are there reoccurring themes or motifs in my image selections?

◁ △ **Collecting scraps** Inspiration books serve as a vessel in which to store anything that triggers a creative reaction. Before mounting, arrange the images that relate to each other so each spread has a cohesive mood and direction.

UNIT 9
design considerations

Creating cohesion through motif, silhouette, and fabric provides designers with clarity and focus, and there are various ways of achieving this cohesion.

▽ **Motif rhythms** Motif serves to provide a design foundation and unify a collection. The arc and linear design elements of this grouping vary in placement, scale, and fabric through two-dimensional and three-dimensional details.

Motif

Motif is an element that is often repeated in a collection to create unity. It may be a particular shape, a concept, or even a physical element. Motif helps visually unify a group and gives the viewer a sense of narration. Designers often implement motif in a variety of ways within a collection to prevent redundancy and monotony.

The intricacies of a butterfly wing, Moorish tile work, the paper cutouts of Henri Matisse, and the architecture of Zaha Hadid are all examples of shape-oriented motifs that provide rich references through their styles of shape and associated color palettes.

Color

Color often gives the first impression of your collection. It is emotional, and you only need to reference art history to see how powerful color can be to convey a mood and message. How do you feel when you view the soft pastels of Claude Monet, the saturated brights of Henri Matisse, or the bold graphics of Franz Kline? Artists have always used color to support and define emotion, and designers do the same. View artwork throughout history in a museum so you can study the diversity of color usage.

Methods for using shape as motif include the following:

2D
- Seaming shapes/details
- Sweater stitches via texture and/or intarsia
- Beading layouts through color and/or blocked shape
- Print development as all-overs or placed graphics
- Embroideries
- Beading layouts
- Insets
- Topstitching

3D
- Garment silhouette
- Pocket and pocket flap shapes
- Collar and lapels
- Appliqués
- Hemline shapes
- Cuff and placket design
- Cutouts and openings for positive/negative space
- Trims (such as buttons or zipper pulls)
- Accessories

Whereas some designers, such as Dries Van Noten and Marni, use simple shapes to support their color wizardry in textile and graphics design, others, such as Francisco Costa of Calvin Klein, use a more harmonious palette to pronounce construction and detailing. Other designers, such as Rei Kawakubo and Yohji Yamamoto, use the same palette season to season (black and white) to neutralize their message, explore innovation, and allow for a gradual evolution of their artistic development.

An example for how fabric, color, and silhouette create harmony is often seen in eveningwear. One designer might use a fabric that is beaded all over and in many colors, and another may wish to use a fabric that is solid black. A strapless sheath may work best for the beaded fabric, because the design is chiefly about the fabric's texture and design, whereas the solid black fabric may be best in a more silhouette-driven design, as the fabric is a blank canvas. An unsuccessful design would involve the all-over beaded fabric in a highly manipulated and sculptural silhouette, since color and silhouette would compete with each other. Choose one statement, and let the other play a supportive role.

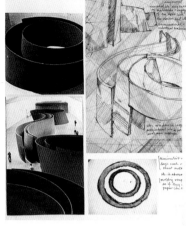

△ ▷ ▽ **Degrees of separation**
Fossilized textures and forms provide this accessory group with a solid foundation for interpretation. The avoidance of literal interpretation results in a highly sophisticated design for the urban customer.

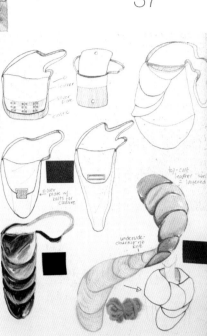

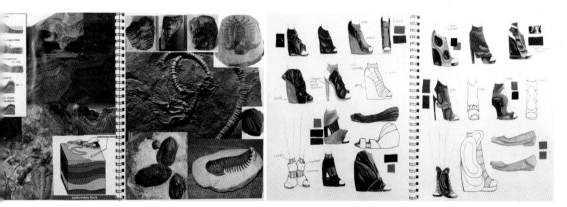

USING MOTIFS IN YOUR WORK:

• Use motif in different scales from look to look.
• Place motif references on different areas of the body to move the viewer's eye.
• Use motif with varied color applications, such as contrast color—for example, a print that uses several colors—and noncolor—for example, seaming shape or a self-on-self fabric appliqué.

• Use texture to convey motif, such as a sweater using a contrast stitch within a blocked-out shape in the base stitch.
• Consider using solid shapes to reference your motif, as well as contour line—for example, prints and graphics.
• Innovate new ways to use motif so your collection maintains a rich depth of design.

MOOD AND COLOR

Explore your options and understand your choices by asking yourself some fundamental questions:

• How do you feel when you view the work?
• What is the scale of color, and how does this elicit emotion?
• How does the scale of the artwork convey a mood?
• How would another color palette change the mood by using different relationships? Graphic? Tonal?
• What is the artist trying to say with color? With shape?
• How would the mood change if the paint was applied differently? Would it be more controlled? More spontaneous?
• Would your emotions change if the artwork was twice as large or twice as small? Why?

Texture and Form

To successfully synthesize your inspiration, design, and aesthetic, a well-merchandised fabric story is essential. Fabrics give a collection its framework, whether merely to support the garment's silhouette, or as the primary "voice" of the garment's design.

Well-balanced collections feature an array and extremity of fabric weights and textures. Through diversity, silhouettes can vary from the tailored and structured to the more fluid and organic. Varied weights also give sequence during a runway presentation when the more tailored, monochromatic silhouettes are shown first, followed by the more silhouette-driven, textured, and graphic looks, and ending with the cocktail/eveningwear, which can be either but gives the audience the "wow" factor of the extreme silhouette, color, texture, shine, or all of the above! It is the "exclamation point" at the end of the show.

Fabric and silhouette should never play equally in a design. Always let one dominate, and allow the other to play a supporting role; otherwise they will compete for attention.

△ **Knitted placements** Graphic, sculptural knit samples are considered for well-designed placement. Testing texture and graphic design to scale is essential when considering silhouette and proportion emphasis.

FOLLOW THESE BASIC GUIDELINES WHEN WORKING WITH FABRIC:

- Diversify fabric weights and/or textures within each of the categories listed.

- Use a selection of solids, patterns, and prints.

- Organize your fabrics by category to ensure you have enough in each, then arrange the fabrics from left to right in order of lineup so you can see color and texture, flow and balance.

△ **Texture extremities** The lack of complex color relationships relies on diverse texture, fabric weights, and graphic proportions to create dynamic interest. The stripe motif is carried through many of the swatches in varying degrees of texture.

The most important rule when using fabric and form is never to force the fabric. Let it do what it wants to do naturally, and show off its best attributes. If the fabric is shiny, such as charmeuse, create volume and drape to let the light reflect it best. If it is transparent and airy, like chiffon, create silhouettes that are voluminous and catch the air to maximize its weightless character. When evaluating fabric for form, before you design, unroll it from the bolt in the fabric store so you can get a sense of volume, drape, and possible construction.

A successful fabric story for a six–eight "look" (or outfit) capsule collection could be as follows:

- Two to three coating weights
- Two to three suiting/jacket weights
- Two to three shirt/blouse weights
- Two to four sweater/jersey weights
- Two to four novelty fabrics

◁ **Textile juxtaposition**
Mixtures of fabric texture and weight complement this group's innovative silhouette development and well-rounded merchandising. By juxtaposing textures and weights, a designer creates looks that can coordinate for various occasions.

◁ **Weight marries form**
The development for this group, using the fabric story to the left, is well considered through silhouette, pattern usage, and fabric placement. Combining appropriate weights and pattern scales with suitable forms ensures that design intention is realized.

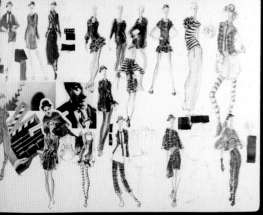

UNIT 10

influences on fashion design

Elements of architecture, ethnic styles, historical costume, art, nature, and technology can all influence designers.

Historical Fashion

Perhaps one of the most common themes designers use for inspiration is historical fashion. Period silhouettes, details, fabrics, finishing techniques, and even the cultural attitude associated with a particular era can all be material from which a collection is conceived. The History of Fashion section (see pages 12–13) describes the evolutions and revolutions that have occurred in society and how these affected dress, silhouettes, fabrics, colors, wearability, and even access to fashion.

The elements that make period garments so suitable to designing for today's market are the immediacy of the subject matter in material that may be extrapolated—such as color, fabric, and silhouette—and how unrelated their context can be to today's fashion, particularly those periods preceding the twentieth century. This allows designers to interpret their researched period in a highly unique and personal manner. For example, how would designers with different aesthetics, such as Versace and Ralph Lauren, interpret the ornate belle époque period of the late nineteenth century? How would fabrics differ? Colors? Silhouettes? Textures?

◁ **Designer chemistry** The Countess of Castiglione, eighteenth-century menswear, the baroque period, and parachutes are all suggested in this look from Junya Watanabe. Diverse exposures and references allow designers to create unique work.

PRACTICAL CONSIDERATIONS

- Be aware of different styles from the period you're researching. For example, the 1960s saw the clean lines and forms of Cardin's and Courrèges' "space age" fashion as well as the more textured and patterned hippie fashions.

- Identify some icons of the period. Their colorful personalities can often provide a foundation for the mood of your collection. (See Assignment 3 on pages 100–101.)

- Notice similarities in decades and the societal forces that drove them. For example, London fashions of the 1920s and the 1960s were similar because of the focus on youth culture. A less curvaceous and "boyish" silhouette ideal, clean lines, and carefree attitude were hallmarks for both generations.

- Adapt your research to today's needs, aspirations, and consumer demands. To be too literal may result in collections appearing too "costume-y" and irrelevant to your customer's needs.

△ **Big band swing** Historical silhouettes combined with modern fabrics and techniques update fashion for today. A specific period may be referenced by a designer, but literal interpretations fail to entice consumers.

PRACTICAL CONSIDERATIONS

When designing from architecture, consider the following physical and conceptual elements:

Physical

- What is the color palette?
- How are color accents used?
- What are the interior/exterior textures? How do they interact?
- What are the macro and micro details?
- How is line used?
- How does line relate both two-dimensionally and three-dimensionally?
- How are shapes used, and what are their relationships?
- How is light integrated or omitted?
- What types of negative space are created?

Conceptual

- How does this building reflect a culture?
- What is the concept and message of the structure to the community?
- How did the form's design advance architecture?
- How does form relate to function?
- How do you feel when you are inside and outside the space?
- Is the structure commenting on society, or challenging it?
- How does the structure relate to its surroundings? Does it blend in?
- How can the architect's concepts for the building serve as your concept for a collection?

Architecture

Architectural inspirations provide designers with limitless styles, periods, colors, forms, textures, concepts, and purposes. From such extremes in architectural styles as the Palace of Versailles, which exemplifies the ornate baroque period and served to represent the economic success of France, to Philip Johnson's Glass House, which is a study of pure geometric form and reductive ornamentation exemplifying the Bauhaus teachings, iconic architecture offers a highly unadulterated point of view proposed by the architect, which can be translated into fashion, both physically and conceptually.

▷ **Origami orientation** The stiff yet lightweight silks for this dramatic silhouette suggest architectural forms while "rain splatter" softens the crisp look. By abstracting an inspiration, the collection will remain highly personal and as unique as the designer's thumbprint.

▷ **Inspiration framework** The structure of a water tower inspired the collection below. Strict lines juxtaposed with an interior and exterior skeleton are accentuated by the organic curve.

▽ **Linear connections** The lack of complex color relationships keeps the focus on design construction and shape motif. Using diverse weights and textures of white fabric creates interest in proportions, directions, and scales of linear motif.

Crafts

Crafted objects are historical and cultural artifacts that often begin life with utilitarian purposes in mind, but can become art forms that are highly descriptive of the time period they were created in and serve as cultural representations of the society that developed them. From the ornate basket weaving and painted pottery of Native Americans, to the furniture of the American Arts and Crafts movement of the early part of the twentieth century, to the contemporary glass art made by Dale Chihuly, crafted objects are products of skill and artistic expression that help define and enrich a community.

▽△ **Cohesion for clarity** Nothing makes a collection hold together more successfully than a motif that is used in various ways. The repeated forms and accents give solidity to this group inspired by Ludwig Schaffrath.

These crafts are commonly found in most cultures and time periods:

- Basketry
- Weaving and textile arts
- Pottery and ceramics
- Furniture design/making
- Metalwork
- Fiber crafts
- Needlework
- Glass art

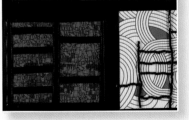

△ **Thematic treatments** Fabric prints, textures, and treatments can be successfully developed, particularly when the inspiration is graphically oriented. Maximize motif development through varied scales, color relationships, fabric weights, and textures.

PRACTICAL CONSIDERATIONS

When researching specific crafts for inspiration, it is helpful to understand how a society's history and fashion history reflect one another, because all forms of design are linked by the zeitgeist present during their creation. For example, the discoveries and interest in space exploration during the 1960s resulted in fashion and product design that was clean in line, and organic and simple in form.

When synthesizing your research with your design process, consider the following questions:

- How can the object's method of production inform design?
- How can color and texture determine fabric choices and relationships?

- Are there unique cultural or societal aspects that may further inform your inspiration and aid in the design process?
- If your craft is cross-cultural, how can the combination of historical or cultural identities merge and create a hybrid that redefines the iconography?
- How can the utilitarian aspects of the craft relate conceptually to design decisions?
- If the craft's form has evolved historically within the particular culture you are referencing, how can the ideas that promoted change relate to the evolution of the collection and design process?

Ethnic Costume

Similar to historical fashion, ethnic costume offers rich and diverse inspirations for design, because the histories of regional dress, and the particularity to the respective society, often provide meanings behind the design, such as political, religious, and sociological identification. Even within cultures that may have proximity to one another, the desire to identify geographic and cultural boundaries through dress has given communities national pride.

The "costume" aspect of traditional ethnic dress, such as samurai armor, traditional Tibetan textiles, and the body adornment of indigenous Amazonian tribes, also provides designers with a wealth of visual material to extrapolate and design from in a highly personalized manner, as the references obtained are often incongruous with today's contemporary fashion design. This allows the individual aesthetics of designers to frame and manipulate the research in a way that best suits their identities and their customers' needs.

▷ **Secrets of the Hermitage** Frequently using cultural references to give narrative to his work, Jean-Paul Gaultier emphasizes the season's themes through highly representational design.

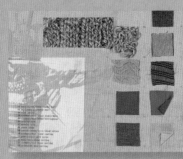

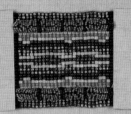

△ **Tones and textures**
A harmonious color palette serves as the basis for a beading layout based on samurai armor. By keeping color relationships tonal, design emphasis can be placed on extreme proportions, silhouettes, and fabric treatments.

△ **Urban samurai** Using both literal and suggested armor details creates a balance of looks for a well-merchandised collection. A consistent silhouette provides emphasis for tonal relationships, design details, and fabric juxtaposition.

PRACTICAL CONSIDERATIONS

When researching ethnic costume, focus on what makes the costume iconographic and particular to the culture by examining color, textures, motif, and silhouette.

- What is the lifestyle of the culture?
- Look at garments used for daywear and those for special ceremonies or occasions. Can you identify unique fabric weights and textures?
- Consider culturally significant colors and their relationships. What quantities of colors are used? Are they tonal or graphics?
- Are iconic prints, patterns, and/or embroideries used to help define the cultural aesthetic?

- Which fabric treatments, manipulations, usages, and dyeing techniques are used?
- Look at silhouettes and garment construction.
- Study the trims, closures, and hardware.
- What accessories are used and what is their unique purpose to the culture?
- What makes this costume unique and iconic to the culture in question?
- How can design elements be adapted for a modern consumer?
- What type of customer would respond to an abstracted representation or a closer translation?
- Will the garment's original purpose alter, and how will this affect design choices when adapting it?

The Street

Street fashion came into prominence during the 1960s when designers wanted to express the deeper political mood of the time and the social changes that were occurring. In an effort to seduce the younger generation, designers such as Yves Saint Laurent launched more affordable, ready-to-wear collections that often recontextualized styles originally meant for utilitarian use; his iconic safari shirt (see below) and peacoat are such examples. As these types of "approachable" fashions were elevated to designer price-point context and gained popularity, the new and fashionable "youthquake" generation no longer felt marginalized from the stratified and regimented worlds of fashion that their mothers were a part of and that they were now questioning and rebelling against.

Today's designers often reference street fashion so that they may employ ideas or images that are connected to their youth-obsessed customer. Prominent examples of designers' street-based inspirations include Vivienne Westwood's interpretations of the punk and new romantic movements of the 1970s and '80s. Karl Lagerfeld has used rap iconography to bring a fresh perspective to the traditional aesthetic at Chanel. Marc Jacobs freely uses street culture in his various collections; his famous spring/summer 1993 Grunge collection for Perry Ellis that was based on the Seattle music scene of the same time period is highly representative of how a design house attempted to connect with an iconic youth movement.

△ **Graffiti diary** Inspired by urban graffiti, the prints for this collection are biographical with each representing a member of the designer's family. When print development is the statement, silhouette and construction must remain simple to avoid competing for emphasis.

▷ **YSL safari** Street fashion comments on historical, societal, and cultural attitudes. Yves Saint Laurent's appropriation of the safari shirt for his collection paved the way for other designers to address the attitudes of a rising youth culture.

PRACTICAL CONSIDERATIONS

It is essential to use your street influence in a suggestive manner. Being too literal can result in a collection that is a parody of your inspiration, and not reflective of current fashion and consumer needs.

Bear in mind the following concepts when researching street iconography:

- Consider your customer. A 1980s "new wave" inspiration will elicit a nostalgic response for someone who lived through the movement, as opposed to others who were not yet born in the '80s.
- Identify the symbols or visual clues that communicate the location and concept.
- Analyze the context and purpose of the clothing from the researched location.
- Focus on the fashion "tribe" that appropriated this style and analyze their demographic profile.
- How can the specificity of the "tribe's" physical space further enhance the mood and design via motif, prints, color relationships, texture, and fabric?
- How can your researched visual clues translate into the contemporary context of fashion?
- What concepts or ideals of the group can inform design choices?

△ **Control, alt, delete** The physical designs of technology can provide inspiration for intarsia sweaters, beading layouts, and fabric juxtapositions as seen in this fall/winter group. Color, texture, and scale are varied to move the eye while maintaining cohesion.

Technology

This is an area that is slowly proving its application to fashion to be limitless; technology has made designers rethink the function of a garment, how production methods can innovate design, and how a seemingly unrelated technical area can influence fashion aesthetically.

Technology's relationship with fashion design contains a breadth of applications, including smart textiles that may some day adjust to the weather, garments that contain wearable technology, concepts and inspirations that reflect the human condition, new methods of production that can create design details—such as laser cutting—and the mapping of more efficient and sustainable methods for producing fashion.

Designers such as Hussein Chalayan and Nicolas Ghesquière for the House of Balenciaga often use technology and futurism as sources of inspiration. Ghesquière's spring 2007 collection for the House of Balenciaga imagined a combination of woman and machine, and Chalayan often examines our interaction with machines and the processes that we invented but that in many ways surpass us in ability.

PRACTICAL CONSIDERATIONS

As fashion designers it can be useful to ask ourselves, "What effect does technology have on our psyche or our paths as human beings?"

It is important to remember that technological inspirations aren't strictly relegated to one particular area, so consider the following contexts of technology in fashion design:

• How can advanced production methods create new design?

• How can areas of technology not yet related to fashion be employed in production, design, or for use within a garment?

• How can these applications produce new textiles and silhouettes?

• What types of technology can increase a garment's function?

• How can technology's physical aspects and aesthetics be used for motif, color, and design?

• What concepts surrounding our relationship with technology can influence a collection?

◁ **Remote robotics** Approaching technology through highly theoretical applications to fashion demonstrates the maximum capabilities for synthesizing two disparate worlds. Hussein Chalayan's exploration of such extreme applications may one day be filtered into more meaningful and practical usages.

Nature

The inspirational and visual material that can be acquired from nature is limitless. Virtually every color, texture, form, and pattern exists naturally and can provide possibilities for well-developed collections.

Nature has served as inspiration for Frank Lloyd Wright and his horizontal architecture that blended in with the plains of the American Midwest, the furniture and set designs conceived by artist Isamu Noguchi, the color palettes for preindustrialized fabric production that relied on the elements for dyes and pigments, and the anthropological forms sculpted by jewelry designer Robert Lee Morris.

△ **She sells seashells** The simple shapes used for childrenswear demand detail-rich garments and whimsical colors to generate excitement. When using an accent color, let its allocation vary to create a rhythm in the presentation.

PRACTICAL CONSIDERATIONS

Given all that nature encompasses, it helps to research in a methodical manner.

- Begin in the library to avoid the pitfalls of using solely what is familiar to you and your surroundings.

- Have a generalized color palette in mind.

- Analyze how and where your initial research arc relates to various forms and colors. If several, filter down to one area so that your motif, color, textures, and silhouettes begin to evoke the unique aspect and mood of your inspiration.

- When developing silhouettes, consider your customers' relationship to your inspiration. How literal must the context of silhouette to nature be?

- Consider the relationships of colors and how these convey the unique personality and identity of your research. How do the researched shapes of color inform design decisions such as print, texture and fabric manipulation, motif, garment construction, and the layering of items?

- To communicate the theme clearly, investigate what gives your inspiration identity. By employing contextual elements specific to your area, you may find that you not only add clarity, but also increase your research to add depth to the collection.

Film and Pop Culture

Since the 1960s, film and pop culture have gone hand in hand. *Desperately Seeking Susan*, which gave New York City's Lower East Side style to teenagers all over the world; *American Gigolo*, which starred Richard Gere and put his followers in the soft tonal colors designed by Armani; Woody Allen's *Annie Hall*, which starred Diane Keaton and made women look sexy in menswear; and *Sex and the City*, which depicted the bond between successful working women and designer labels are all evidence of the power of a style fabricated and marketed by Hollywood or Madison Avenue, creating legions of "wannabes" all over the world.

Pop culture has often garnered accolades on the runway, and many a designer's style has been repositioned and adapted by the general public who often strive to mimic their Hollywood idols. Some design houses have even built a loyal following because of their consistent interpretations of gowns seen on the Academy Awards' red carpet, so that their customers may identify with a particular actress' style, whereas other designers have become household names, not for their creations, but because of the stars who wear them.

Celebrity icons and their stylists spread trends through Hollywood exposure to mainstream audiences who wish to emulate the look.

PRACTICAL CONSIDERATIONS

When using film or pop culture as inspiration, consider the aspects of styling that create a sense of iconography.

• Study the choice of color, lighting, props, scenery, and various other visual cues to help you identify both a particular mood and a more focused area of research to expand upon.

◁ **Silver screen icons**
Period dress, whimsical charm, and modern proportions all collide to develop a collection based on Charlie Chaplin's film *The Little Tramp*. The character's awkwardness influenced the collection's unconventional proportions and construction.

UNIT 11
color

The history, culture, and psychology of color have profoundly complex relationships.

How a society forms meaning around color ranges from the natural, the religious, the political, to the purely emotional. Often, meanings can vary from culture to culture with uniquely defined symbolism; red in Chinese culture conveys good luck and prosperity, whereas Western societies sense danger when using the color on road signs. Colors that denote mourning range from yellow in Egypt, to black in America, blue in Iran, red in South Africa, and purple in Thailand.

Frequently, our contemporary associations of color stem from history; blue was worn by ancient Roman public servants and has thus been appropriated to the police uniform today, and purple is considered a royal color because of sumptuary laws enacted in ancient times that allowed only nobility to wear the costly color that was laboriously extracted from a seashell found in the Mediterranean.

As well as individual colors, color combinations can also carry cultural meaning. Red and green have long symbolized the Christmas holiday; red, white, and blue in many cultures represent patriotism and, to some degree, conservatism; red, orange, yellow, and brown signal the seasonal change to fall and Thanksgiving in the United States; white and navy have long been associated with nautical themes; and the combination of yellow with red is often used in restaurants to psychologically produce feelings of hunger in patrons.

▷ **Color blocks** Designers use color to accentuate the mood and theme of their collections. The bold, solid shapes of saturated color in this collection emphasize the sculptural shapes and seaming details.

COLORS AND THEIR FREQUENTLY ASSOCIATED MEANINGS:

White Purity, surrender, truth, peace, innocence, simplicity, sterility, coldness, death, marriage (Western cultures), birth, virginity

Black Intelligence, rebellion, mystery, modernity, power, sophistication, formality, elegance, evil, death, slimming quality (fashion), occult

Gray Elegance, conservatism, respect, wisdom, old age, boredom, dullness, pollution, neutrality, formality, blasé, decay, military, education, strength

Red Passion, strength, energy, sex, love, romance, speed, danger, anger, revolution, wealth (China), marriage (India)

Orange Happiness, energy, balance, heat, enthusiasm, playfulness, warning, fall, desire, optimism, Protestantism, abundance

Yellow Joy, happiness, summer, cowardice, illness, hazards, greed, femininity, friendship. (During a time of war, yellow ribbons symbolize the hope for troops to return home.)

Green Nature, fertility, youth, inexperience, environment, wealth, generosity, jealousy, illness, greed, growth, health, stability, calming, new beginnings

Blue Water, oceans, peace, unity, calmness, coolness, confidence, conservatism, loyalty, dependability, idealism, depression, sadness

Purple Nobility, envy, spirituality, creativity, mystery, wisdom, gaudiness, exaggeration, confusion, pride, instability

Brown Nature, richness, rusticism, tradition, boorishness, dirt, dullness, filth, heaviness, poverty, roughness, earth, comfort

COLOR THEORY

Learning the fundamentals of color theory will give you a solid foundation from which to communicate your ideas and concepts successfully in two- and three-dimensional formats. Although designers don't select color palettes based on the "science" of color, it is important to understand basic relationships that can create maximum results, particularly when mixing paints or other media to illustrate your designs.

Primary colors Red, yellow, and blue. These are colors that cannot be created by combining any other colors or hues. Primaries are used to create all other colors.

Secondary colors Green, orange, and purple. These are created directly from a combination of two primary colors.

Tertiary colors Yellow-orange, red-orange, red-purple, blue-purple, blue-green, and yellow-green. These are formed by mixing a primary and secondary color.

Complementary colors Red/green, orange/blue, and purple/yellow. Two colors that are opposite each other on the color wheel. Placing complementary colors next to each other makes for maximum vibrancy.

Analogous colors Colors that are next to each other on a twelve-part color wheel.

Tints Colors mixed with white.

Shades Colors mixed with black.

Tone A general term to describe the level of shade or tint.

Hue The particular gradation, or the variety of the color.

Patina The surface or texture of the color, often associated with the aging process.

Chroma The purity of a color in relation to gray.

Saturation The purity and density of a color.

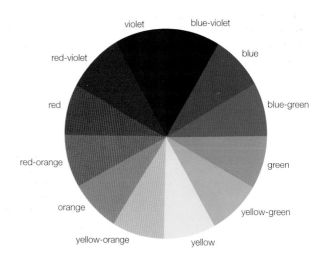

Seasonal Colors

Fashion designers often rely on a palette of colors traditionally associated with the different selling seasons or deliveries. Colors, along with silhouettes, fabrics, and textures, help to signal a change of season and entice consumers to buy. Many designers work within a fabric palette for the particular delivery, and care is given to how the changing colors flow into one another on the sales floor from delivery to delivery. For example, an accent color such as ruby red in the first fall delivery, which sits alongside core colors such as camel and charcoal, may reappear and be more dominant in the second delivery, when the core colors change to navy and ivory.

▽ **Moroccan kasbah** Weathered hues and natural fabrics contribute to the relaxed feeling in this warm-weather menswear collection. Summer collections often use light colors to reflect the sun and appear cool to the customer.

COLORS THAT ARE OFTEN USED AS SEASONAL COLORS, NOT NECESSARILY ALL IN THE SAME COLLECTION:

Transition Brown, olive green, pumpkin, cranberry, ochre yellow, dark khaki, charcoal gray, taupe, black, chocolate brown, deep rich colors

Holiday Metallics such as silver, gold, and bronze; champagne; ivory; black; jewel tones such as sapphire blue, ruby red, emerald green

Resort/pre-spring Soft pastels, white, navy blue, cherry red, bright green, tan

Spring Bright colors such as yellow, kelly green, indigo, purple, navy, light khaki

Summer White, bright saturated colors

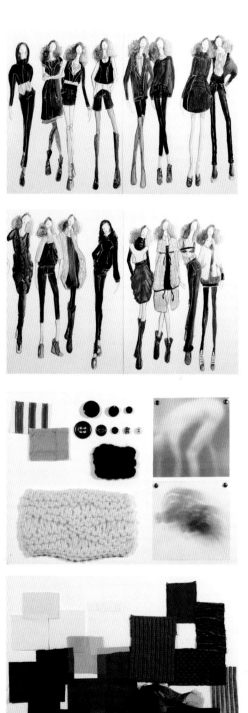

The colors listed in the panel, opposite, are only examples; variations will occur based on trends, the market targeted, and the number of deliveries within a season. For example, designers for the juniors market might stay away from the traditional fall colors of gray or taupe, because their customers don't respond to such a mature palette, preferring brighter colors. Conversely, though a designer may have one gray delivery, a multiple-delivery season in such somber colors may not be appropriate.

Another important exception to this practice is the designer price-point and haute-couture markets. Often these markets supply trend information to lower-priced markets, and may ignore traditional color palettes for the sake of their own vision for the collection.

◁ **Graphic neutrals** Winter collections demand layered looks. Graphic combinations of color throughout the group can give a casual feeling because of the emphasis on mix-and-match pieces. A well-rounded collection offers customers one-stop shopping.

△ **Winter hibernation** Cocoon silhouettes, wrapping, and padded fabrics give warmth and comfort in this highly organic collection. Tonal colors emphasize drape, and tactile fabrics and swaddling proportions give a sophisticated look of protection and security.

◁ ▽ **Looking ahead** Some designers subscribe to trend services that predict which colors will be prevalent in an upcoming season. How designers use such forecasting is very personal; trend predictions may serve as the collection's foundation or as mere accents.

· collection palette ·

· traditional chic palette ·

· lounge/casual palette ·

· color palette ·

Cargo A Go-Go

Fair isle fun

Snow Bunny

essential turtleneck
$58.00 —

fabric >>
☐ herringbone wool
☐ flannel
☐ silk jersey
☐ cashmere
☐ wool

Wool herringbone full skirt
— $98.00 —

$198.00 —

Trend Forecasting

Fashion designers must constantly exercise their "sixth sense" to know how consumer behavior will evolve and what the customer's needs will be. Which colors will be favored? What new silhouettes will appear and how (dis)similar will they be when compared with the previous season's? Will it be a tailored season or a more organic one? Will fabric palettes exhibit graphic color and dramatic texture relationships, or more subtle and tonal color palettes?

To assist designers in their own observations and speculations, forecasting services offer well-formulated research that examines global changes, often through historical, cultural, societal, political, and economic contexts, that will affect fashion.

Trend-forecasting agencies research years in advance for a particular season, and use myriad techniques that center on consumer behavior and global changes, all of which benefit designers when creating collections. Although it is essential to maintain consistency in a brand's identity, it is also critical to maintain currency of design within the ever-shifting fashion climate.

Fashion Trends and Their Relevancy: High or Low?

When considering the relevancy of fashion trends today, and whether a designer will follow them or not, larger concerns must be addressed. It is worth examining the speed at which global issues affect fashion today in contrast with the pre-Internet days; how long trends last and dominate a market may largely reflect the ease of access one has to information the moment it occurs.

Increasingly, shifts in fashion are moving at such a fast pace, season to season, that the moment a trend gains recognition it is replaced by another, thus blurring any significant representation as a truly defined "trend" in the market. Will trends continue to be relevant as the "information highway" gains even more momentum and public access to information is increased?

In a related topic, how has the global market been altered by the heightened sophistication levels of the mass audience that now has access to affordable design? When high-end design houses such as Comme des Garçons design for fast-fashion companies such as H&M, how does this influence product to the mass-market consumer who now has an increased exposure and heightened sense of design? Will designers maintain their loyal following for their high price-point collections when more affordable "designer aesthetic" product is made available to the general public?

AGENCIES

Listed below are some of the most influential and recognized trend-forecasting agencies:

Trend Union

Presided over by Li Edelkoort, Trend Union produces seasonal trend books and audiovisual presentations for the textile and fashion industries. Trend Union also presents for the interior design, retail, and "well-being" markets. Their offices are on five continents, which reveals just how large their presence is in the global design community.

Promostyl

A global trend-forecasting agency with headquarters in Paris, this organization focuses on lifestyle trends by providing research on color and silhouette directions. In existence for almost forty years, the agency is well known for balancing creativity with the commercial, and services such industries as apparel, beauty, and automotive.

Peclers

For almost thirty years Peclers Paris has offered trend-forecasting publications internationally. With offices in New York, Los Angeles, Miami, and Canada, Peclers provides publications that center on consumer needs and wants in the fashion, interior, and industrial design fields.

World Global Style Network

Perhaps one of the most extensive fashion websites, WGSN offers a breadth of information in all fashion design markets and provides current research from around the world. Offices are in London, New York, Los Angeles, Madrid, Cologne, and Tokyo.

Pantone Inc.

One of the world's premier color services, Pantone provides a color system for diverse industries. Frequently used by designers when creating prints or fabric dye lots where a universally known standard must be used, their books are used around the world in areas such as textiles, digital technology, and industrial design.

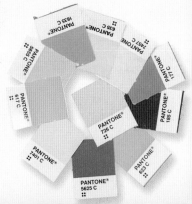

Color as Inspiration

From the burnt umbers, alizarin crimsons, and fiery oranges of the American Southwest, to the sensitive relationships of off-whites seen in a glacier, the colors extrapolated from your research and mood boards will provide the collection not only with color references, but also the proportions in which they are used. Although your images may provide you with a solid foundation for building a palette, care must always be taken when selecting color for its specificity to ensure it complements the wearer, is saleable in the proportion and silhouette it is applied to, and meets the aesthetics of your targeted audience.

COLOR CONTEXTS

When reviewing your research and mood board, analyze the color contexts.

- Which colors serve as the mood board's foundation, and which provide accents?
- How are the foundation and accent colors proportionate to one another?
- How many base colors can be extracted?
- How many accent colors are used? Are they used equally or in varying percentages?
- What moods and emotions do the colors produce and how do they relate to your theme? How can you accentuate this through fabric weight diversity/similarity and silhouette development?
- Does the placement and shape of a color provide inspiration for design?
- How can the tonal differences of an image provide reference for fabric development such as sheer and opaque fabrics, prints and dyeing techniques, layering, and other methods for color manipulation?
- What textures are present and how can they inform textile selection? What are the proportions of textures shown? How can texture be used as an accent?

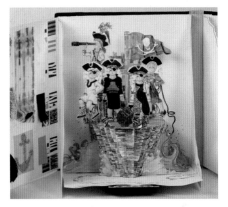

△ **Pop-up pirates** Using a presentation format that highlights the design category, this childrenswear group uses complex print and color relationships in heavily layered looks.

▷ **Material worth** The color story of blue, green, and white is given interest through extensive fabric and print development.

◁ **Masai elements** Tribal colors, textures, and fabric treatments appeal to a sophisticated, urban customer. Consider how inspiration can be suggested through iconic color relationships.

▽ **Fire codes** Direct color references, materials, and hardware give these firefighter-inspired accessories originality and charm.

PRACTICAL CONSIDERATIONS

To develop color palettes based on relationships in the mood board, there are a number of processes you can follow.

Consider the customer

Although a particular color may look great in a painting, on a piece of furniture, or even within a wallpaper pattern, color that is worn becomes part of the wearer's physicality and personality.

Consider color scale

A bright yellow may be appropriate in a large silhouette, such as a trench coat, for one designer, but another may find it appropriate for use only as a small accent in a print or lining. Sometimes it isn't the color that seems inappropriate, but the contexts surrounding it.

Define the color relationships

When considering which core fabrics will create the foundations of your collection, define these colors and tones first to provide a foundation for all others. Shades of beige, gray, black, or navy are common "core colors," and those that are comparatively bright and/or more saturated are frequently used as accents. For some designers, particularly the bridge market, this formula remains fairly consistent for each seasonal delivery, whereas other designers disregard color references from their inspiration and use a familiar palette so they may refine their identity more subtly from season to season.

Thematic and contextual representation

How colors are extrapolated from a mood board to create a palette that conveys the desired feeling relies heavily on their context. How does the color relate to the whole fabric story? Does another color that is similar in tone need to be employed to create a graduation of color? Does a harmonious palette demonstrate the mood best, or one that includes colors that clash and compete for attention?

The "middlemen"

When a fabric palette consists of solid colors that are unrelated and disjointed, it is essential to create a "middleman" to unify them and create a true story. Prints, woven or printed shirting stripes, multicolored embroideries, sweater knits with various colors, and even beading layouts can all serve as an axis to bring unrelated colors together and harmonize the group.

Color Rhythm

As you build collections that are well solved in mood, color palette, motif, fabric weights, and merchandising, begin to consider how color accents and the general palette will flow from look to look, and how items may be coordinated together, particularly for sportswear, where the concept of mix-and-match is essential.

Color proportion, placement, and fabric must vary from look to look so that you give your customer options for how items will work together. For some looks, the accent color can be used as a very small element that may not be part of the garments at all, such as a purse. In other looks, the accent color can be used to give your customer versatility of color proportion, such as a cashmere sweater that can be worn under a jacket for a sliver of color, or on its own for a bolder effect. The accent color can also be employed in prints or as a sweater yarn that is twisted with other muted colors for a less intense effect, or in a novelty fabric such as silk chiffon for eveningwear, when large proportions of color are frequently used for dramatic effect.

▷ **The grand finale** How you finish the collection's presentation could either crescendo at the end in large, extreme proportions of color, or create a full-circle effect by relating to the use of color at the beginning of the lineup.

PRACTICAL CONSIDERATIONS

Ask the following questions when analyzing the color rhythm of your collection:

• How will proportion of color create momentum as the collection progresses?

• How does the proportion of color used relate to the item? Is it a layering piece, an accessory, outerwear, core item, or novelty item? How does this address the customer's needs?

• Does the level of color saturation need to be adjusted for the larger pieces or for the smaller layering or accent pieces?

• How can color be used as a solid and in a pattern to vary its visual impact?

• Does the color palette keep the collection unified on the sales floor?

• How does color change in different fabric textures? Is it heightened in one and lessened in another?

• How can color shape or placement be used as a motif to create cohesion?

◁ **Compare** When composing your finalized layout of figures or "looks," working from left to right, analyze how the accent color is used in proportion and placement on the body. Designers frequently do this when they compose their model lineup, also called the "run-of-show."

◁ **Less to more**
Build momentum of color proportion as you move through the looks, so that the percentage of color used and its placement always varies. Like motif, it keeps the collection unified, particularly on the sales floor.

UNIT 12
fabrics & fibers

The importance of choosing the right fabric and/or fiber for your design cannot be underscored enough.

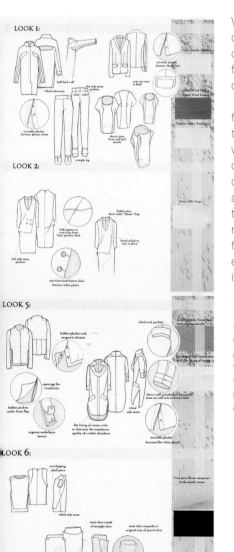

Whereas materials provide the practical needs of supporting silhouette and construction, fabric choice can affect every aspect of your collection, from concept to form, customer, mood, and design cohesion.

Listed on the following pages are well-known fabrics that are frequently used in virtually all markets today. Although the types of fabric weaves and weights available are seemingly limitless, those detailed will provide you with a solid foundation of fabric knowledge. It is important to note that although they have been grouped by the category they are often associated with, there are no solid rules to a fabric's usage. For some designers, for example, silk chiffon may be an exclusively eveningwear fabric, while others may incorporate it into their daywear.

◁ **Puzzle pieces** Harmonizing fabric weights with intended silhouettes is an art that takes much experience to master. Draping the proposed fabric from its bolt into the desired silhouette on the body ensures accurate selection.

▷ **Know your categories** Always group fabrics on swatch cards by category to ensure that a successful merchandising plan is created. Though some fabrics may overlap categories, decide where their emphasis will be in the collection.

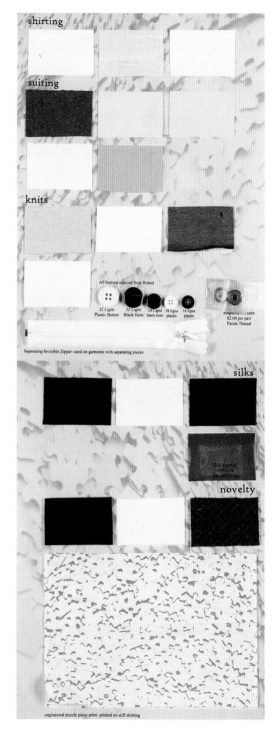

Daywear

Wool gabardine
Tightly woven fabric known for its durability and versatility. The use of 100 percent worsted wool gives a smooth appearance on one side and twill on the reverse. Traditionally used in menswear suiting, but now a mainstay across all categories.

Tropical wool
Lightweight worsted wool commonly used for suiting during transitional seasons.

Cotton poplin
Medium- to heavyweight fabric most frequently made of cotton or cotton/polyester blend. This sturdy fabric with noticeable ridges is used in casual sportswear for men and women, particularly for shirting.

Denim
Woven cotton twill fabric of medium weight, originally used for workwear. Today it is generally used as bottoms and jackets for more casual garments.

Chambray
Lightweight woven fabric combining a colored yarn with an undyed yarn in a plain weave to create a denim look. Used for casual sportswear for men and women.

Corduroy
Durable fabric with parallel lengthwise cords or ridges called "wales." The thickness of the wales determines the fabric's use; thinner wales give a softer feel ideal for shirts; thicker wales for bottoms and jackets.

Broadcloth
Densely woven fabric that is extremely sturdy and very soft. Originally wool, it is now made in cotton and is perfect for shirts and blouses.

Voile
Lightweight sheer fabric with a gauze-like quality made of silk, rayon, or cotton. Often used in lingerie, baby clothes, blouses, and skirts.

Lawn
Plain-weave, semitransparent fabric originally made from linen but now made from combed cotton, resulting in a silky hand feel. Crisper than voile but less crisp than organdy, it is suitable for blouses.

Organdy
Typically 100 percent cotton, a crisp, transparent woven fabric often used in shirts and blouses.

Batiste
Delicate, fine cotton with a graceful drape perfect for baby clothing, lingerie, and nightgowns.

Cotton sateen
Medium-weight fabric, made from mercerized cotton, with a similar sheen to satin. Its high thread count makes it soft to the touch and perfect for casual separates.

Cavalry twill
Strong cotton, wool, or worsted fabric constructed in double twill, which results in diagonal, subtle ridges that give it a distinct look. Traditionally used for pants and jackets.

Gabardine
Tightly woven, durable twill with a distinct diagonal ridge running throughout, commonly used in pants and rainwear for men and women.

Swiss dot
Sheer cotton fabric often made of lawn or batiste with a small dot pattern either woven into the fabric or flocked onto the surface. Typically used in shirting, dresses, and children's clothing.

Linen
Summer-weight fabric (made from flax plant) with natural slubs running throughout. Known for its tendency to crease, which is part of its charm, it is available in various weights for separates.

Corduroy

Cotton sateen

Organdy

Linen

Canvas, duck, sailcloth

Very stiff, durable, plain fabrics (typically cotton), suitable for outerwear. Although dyeable, these traditionally come in unbleached white.

Chino

Twill fabric made from mercerized cotton and typically khaki in color. Originally used for army uniforms but has become a staple today for men's and women's pants.

Chintz

Boldly patterned fabric of flowers, abstract geometrics, or figures, traditionally made from 100 percent cotton. Finishes vary from coarse and rough to smooth and glossy. Originally used in upholstery; used today in separates.

Waffle weave

Woven with a recessed square pattern reminiscent of waffles—hence the name. Often 100 percent cotton but may be offered in blends; used in casual and athletic clothing.

Challis

Lightweight, plain-weave fabric, made from cotton or wool, usually with a printed design. Its soft hand feel makes it perfect for pajamas, dresses, and blouses.

Tailored

Camel hair

May be made from 100 percent camel hair or camel hair blended with wool. Colors aren't usually dyed but remain neutral. This classic fabric has a fine, brushed, hairlike finish, traditionally used in coating or suits.

Wool felt

Nonwoven fabric created when the sheep's wool or fiber is subjected to heat, moisture, or agitation, creating a very thick, dense fabric used in outerwear, coats, and jackets.

Zibeline

Soft, airy fabric with a long, glossy pile from a mixture of mohair-type fibers with a twill weave. Long-defined nap lies in one direction, adding structure and body, and making it ideal for suits and coats requiring extensive tailoring.

Sharkskin

Smooth, unique weave using a blend of rayon or acetate along with wool in white with colored fibers to create a basket-weave effect. Its two-toned woven appearance makes it popular for men's and women's suits.

Evening/Bridal

Organza

Plain-weave, sheer fabric, often silk or a synthetic blend, used to create volume in bridal dresses.

Chiffon

Sheer, delicate woven fabric, often 100 percent silk but available in synthetic, used for its fluidity and "airy" quality. Suitable for dresses and blouses.

Georgette

More opaque than chiffon, often made from silk but available in synthetics. Has a crinkly, crepe-like texture and is dry to the touch. Drapes well and is ideal for blouses and dresses.

Charmeuse

Luxury fabric with a glossy satin finish, extremely lightweight. Often made in 100 percent silk, its fluidity creates a soft drape suitable for dresses and separates.

Crepe de Chine

Light, plain-woven fabric, typically 100 percent silk with a slightly crepe character. Used in dresses and blouses.

Crepe-back satin

Lightly textured, two-faced fabric with crepe on one side and a high-luster satin on the other. Available in silk and synthetics, the soft drape is suitable for dresses and blouses.

Canvas

Chintz

Georgette

Organza

Duchesse satin

Elegant fabric, the heaviest within the silk family. Has subtle luster. Often used in couture and for extravagant occasions.

Hammered satin

Thick, lustrous fabric with the sheen of satin and a surface similar to hammered metal. Its drape makes it suitable for elegant dresses, blouses, and special occasion garments.

Taffeta

Historically made from silk, but available today in a variety of synthetics. Has a very tight weave and is known for its stiff, crisp quality, used to create distinct silhouettes, typically for evening- or bridalwear.

Shantung/raw silk

The raw silk fibers used to create this fabric allow the slubs to show and give it a highly textured quality. This provides a durable nubby fabric used in spring and fall collections.

Douppioni (or dupioni)

Shimmering fabric created by weaving threads of rough silk fibers together, giving a crisp drape to the finish.

Moiré

Sometimes referred to as "watered silk" because of the rippling, watered pattern that gives this fabric its distinct look. Made in silk, rayon, or blends; perfect for evening- or bridalwear.

Ottoman faille

Has a faintly ribbed pattern, similar to grosgrain ribbon, creating a textured feel. Available in silk, cotton, and rayon; used in formalwear since it creates stiff, structured silhouettes.

Velvet

Soft, plush fabric made of silk, cotton, or synthetic blends. The threads stick up, forming a soft-to-the-touch pile. Traditionally an evening fabric, but can cross over into daywear.

Lamé

Slinky, brocaded fabric made from interwoven metallic threads, typically gold or silver, that give it a sheen. Used in eveningwear and costume.

Tulle

Lightweight fabric that looks like netting and can be silk, for a draped effect, or synthetic, for a stiffer look. Typically used in bridal veils, ballet tutus, and petticoats.

Peau de soie

Medium- to heavyweight fabric with a satin weave and dull finish. Typically silk but available in polyester, this is traditionally used in bridal and cocktail attire.

Knits

Matte jersey

Dull, flat knit fabric made with fine crepe yarns. Has a crisp, dry feel. Popular for travel or easy-care dresses and separates, it drapes well and transitions well from day to night.

Wool jersey

Medium- to heavyweight, 100 percent wool knit with a subtle drape. Works well for fall/winter in casual separates and dresses.

Silk jersey

Fluid knit with a subtle sheen that can be used in a wide variety of silhouettes. Transitions well from day to evening.

Velour

Plush cotton with a thick nap, making it soft to the touch. Unlike velvet, this knit is highly stretchy and is typically used in casual loungewear and athletic cover-ups.

Boiled wool

Similar to felting, the knitted fabric is boiled, causing it to shrink by approximately 25–30 percent, producing very thick finished goods suitable for structured jackets and coats.

Taffeta

Douppioni

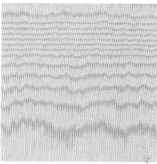
Moiré

Velour

Miscellaneous Novelties

Matelassé
From the French word meaning "quilted/padded" or "cushioned," this heavy, rich textile, commonly made of 100 percent cotton, features hand stitching, in either geometric or floral motifs, that gives the effect of quilting. Originally used in coverlets and bedding, this technique now translates well into outerwear.

Bird's-eye
Medium-weight fabric woven with a pattern of small diamonds, each with a dot in the center.

Mohair
Shorn hair from an angora goat can be knitted or woven. The garment maintains a long-hair finish with a brushed look and is well suited for outerwear pieces. The knitted yarn is used in sweaters.

Damask
Traditionally used in upholstery, this fabric has a dense weave, often 100 percent silk, characterized by a background of lustrous fabric against which raised designs appear—typically geometric or botanicals. Good for outerwear and tailored pieces.

Brocade
Heavy, intricate jacquard made with various types of silk accented with metallic threads.

The fabric was originally used in upholstery but is now popular for costume, stage use, and formal occasions.

Raffia
Taken from palm leaves, this natural fiber can be woven like straw to create a very coarse-textured fabric, typically used in millinery.

Toray® Ultrasuede
Original trademarked microfiber synthetic substitute for suede. Completely machine washable and was introduced to the designer market by Halston in the 1970s.

Houndstooth
Duo-tone fabric with a characteristic broken-check or tooth pattern, traditionally in black and white wool twill. It is traditionally a menswear staple for suits and coats, but is also used in women's suiting.

Glenplaid
Traditional, classic plaid pattern of muted colors or black, gray, and white. Two dark and two light stripes alternate with four dark and four light stripes vertically and horizontally, forming a crossing pattern of irregular checks.

Moleskin
Heavy-napped, cotton twill fabric, used especially in casual tailored looks or lightweight coats.

Chenille
Translated as "caterpillar" in French, this yarn or fabric is made from cotton, rayon, or acrylic. Its deep pile is soft and fuzzy, giving it a distinctive look. Originally used in bedspreads and carpets, it is mainly used for sweaters and jackets in the apparel industry.

Nylon
Strong and lightweight, man-made synthetic fabric made from polyamide. Resists absorbing moisture and dries easily, so is best used in swimwear, activewear, or rainwear.

Bengaline
Woven silk/wool/synthetic blend with fine "ribbed" texture. This two-sided fabric with matte on one side and sheen on the other is ideal for pants with a vertical stretch.

Alpaca
Referring to the hair of Peruvian alpacas, this style of fabric was originally made from alpaca hair but is often now blended with mohair and wool for wovens and knits.

Vicuña
Luxurious fabric softer and warmer than any other wool. Harvested from the vicuña (a relative of the llama), the hair is eight times finer than that of human hair and is used in coats and outerwear.

Damask

Brocade

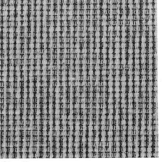
Chenille

Mohair

Cashmere
(knits and wovens)

Obtained from the cashmere goat, this is fine in texture and strong, light, and soft. The fibers can be knitted or woven into the finest luxury products.

Eyelet

Traditionally white cotton, this fabric, as the name suggests, uses cutout holes with embroidered edges to create an overall pattern, and is popular in children's clothing, dresses, and blouses.

Broderie Anglaise

This technique creates patterns and shapes using cutout motifs with embroidery. Traditionally used in undergarments and children's clothing, today it is used in women's dresses and blouses.

Pique

Often cotton, this fabric has a subtle texture often referred to as bird's-eye, and is suitable for dresses and separates.

Gingham

Plain-weave, lightweight cotton using dyed or white and dyed fibers to form checks on a white background. Traditionally a favorite in children's clothing, gingham is used across all categories today.

Seersucker

Lightweight cotton fabric with vertical stripes in a "puckered" effect contrasted by flat areas. Commonly used in men's suits and women's separates.

Terry cloth

Cotton pile fabric known for its softness and high absorbency. Characterized by thick uncut loops, which form a soft pile on both sides of the fabric. Often used in towels and bathrobes, it can also be used in athletic wear.

COMMON TERMS

Jacquard

Textiles with complex patterns, such as brocade, damask, and matelassé. Refers to the mechanical loom invented by Joseph Marie Jaquard in 1801 that was first used to create the complex patterns.

Plissé

Crinkled finish given to cotton and nylon fabrics by treatment with caustic soda solution.

Cloqué

Fabric with an irregularly raised, blistered surface.

Bouclé

Type of yarn, usually three-ply, that has one thread looser than the others, creating a curly looped finish that adds texture to fabric or knits. Often 100 percent wool or synthetic blend, it is used in jackets and suits or sweaters.

Crepe

Crinkly, crimped, or grainy fabric.

Burnout

Known as "devoré" and using a technique similar to etching, a chemical eats away at the fibers, leaving the fabric background behind to create a pattern.

Crushed velvet

Textured finish with the appearance of being crushed/creased.

Panne velvet

Slinky fabric with piles that lie flat, creating a soft hand feel with wonderful drape.

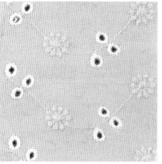

Broderie Anglaise

Gingham

UNIT 13
knitwear

The weights, textures, and design capacity of knitwear are limitless and essential for creating a well-merchandised collection.

Depending on the knit structure and fiber, knitwear can be draped like chiffon, tailored like wool suiting, and even serve as a winter coat. From the gauge sizes of yarn, fibers available, stitches possible, and techniques applied, knitwear is considered by many to be fashion design at its most conceptual and inventive.

The appeal for many designers when designing knitwear is the ability to create the fabric and form from scratch. As a result, the effects and types of forms one can create are tremendous and can suit all aesthetics and categories of design. From sheer cashmere knits often seen at Jil Sander to the rope-like knits designed by Giles Deacon and Alexander McQueen, from the matte jersey eveningwear dresses of Madame Grès that are often referenced by contemporary designers to athletic apparel and the iconic T-shirt, knitwear applies to all categories, price points, ages, and lifestyles.

As a collection develops, it is useful to utilize knitwear for its unique characteristics and ease of wear. From forms that require minimal construction for slim fit to architectural silhouettes that may be more comfortably worn than their woven counterparts, knitwear is often seen as an addition to a designer's collection, particularly when diversifying motif and color relationships. Knitwear may even be the signature and focus of the brand, as seen at houses such as TSE and Missoni. Although the technical aspects for executing knitwear designs require substantial knowledge, having a basic understanding of terms and visual examples associated with the medium will provide you with enough material to begin designing knitwear.

◁▷ **Knitted organics** The range of knitted textures and sculptural forms is limitless in knitwear and is often used to underscore a collection's theme and motif. Rigid wool flannel bands complement the soft texture of this collection based on human anatomy.

◁ **Volume and silhouette** Sweater knits are not just relegated to traditional shapes and weights. The ability to invent knitted fabric, form, and silhouette effects attracts many designers who enjoy its limitless creative possibilities and technical applications.

CORE TERMS

These core knitwear terms will provide you with a foundation for design:

Cut and sew

Garments made with pre-knit yardage. Garment patterns are laid on top, cut, and sewn in a similar way to woven fabrics.

Sweater knits

Unlike pre-knit goods, sweater knits are made on special machines that knit the pattern pieces to their intended shapes. These are then assembled to form the garment.

Knit

The first basic stitch learned in knitting, which forms the front or "right side" of the work.

Purl

The second basic stitch learned in knitting, which forms the back or "wrong side" of the work.

Plain knitting

Knit and purl stitches used together form plain knitting.

Jersey

Formed by knitting one row and purling one row.

Rib

Knit and purl stitches combined in any variety.

Variegated rib

Uneven combination of knit and purl stitches; for example, three by one, five by three, etc.

Engineered rib

Variety of rib stitches used in combination with one another to form the body of the knit garment.

Garter stitch

Every row is knit stitch, giving a reverse jersey look to both sides of the work.

Gauge

Term used to describe the size of yarn: 5gg, 7gg, 12gg, 16gg, and 24gg are most commonly used for machine sizes, and 3gg or 5gg are most commonly used for hand knits. Knitting a sample with your chosen yarn and measuring how many stitches equal one inch and how many rows equal one inch will enable you to map out your pattern. The size of yarn thickness determines gauge.

Marl

Two or more yarns of differing colors or sizes knitted together to create a random pattern or texture. The pattern is visible on the back and front of the work.

Plait

Machine technique used most often with Lurex or metallic yarn. One end of the "novelty" yarn is added along with the base yarn and is knitted only on the face of the work, so as not to create an itchy texture on the inside. The resulting fabric has a similar look to marl.

Cable

Twisted three-dimensional pattern that uses double-ended needles to create vine-like or geometric patterns.

Bobble

Three-dimensional effect created by multiplying stitches from a single stitch and decreasing back down to the original stitch.

Intarsia

Technique used to create multicolored patterns. Shapes are generally large and are knitted as separate pieces that are then fitted together like puzzle pieces to form the garment.

Fair Isle

Technique used to create multiple colored patterns that are generally small in scale. Made by knitting the design into the pattern pieces at the same time. When a yarn color changes, a "float" is created on the wrong side and carried over to where the pattern resumes.

Float

Length of yarn carried over on the back of the work when changing colors.

Jacquard

Machine technique used to emulate intarsia patterns with a limited number of colors in repeat.

Full fashioned

When stitches are transferred over to create shape at armholes, necklines, princess seams, etc.

Full needle rib

Machine double-bed rib that creates the effect of one-by-one rib on both sides of the garment.

Pointelle

Effect created by knitting stitches together in one row, then adding the stitch back in the next knit row to create a hole.

Drop needle or needle out

Transferring one or more stitches onto the adjacent stitch, creating a ladder effect as the yarn is carried over the dropped stitch area on subsequent rows.

Lace

Any amount of lace effects can be created with engineered pointelle patterns.

△ **Light as a feather** As dense as wool coating or as sheer as chiffon, knits span every conceivable weight and purpose. The delicate and sheer quality of knitwear can be enhanced by combining simple stitches with denser areas.

◁ **Explore your options** Croquis pages show how stitch placement and silhouette proportion can work together in varying ways. It is essential to give other versions as you sketch so that other ideas may develop and design options are fully investigated.

BASIC TRIMS AND FINISHING TECHNIQUES:

Self-start
Term used for a full rib body where the rib itself forms the start and no additional trim is necessary. Sometimes a tighter tension is requested for ⅜ in. (1 cm) at the start to hold shape.

Rib
Knit and purl alternated in multiples (one by one, two by two, four by four, etc.).

Tubular
The most common finish used in machine knitting. Jersey is knitted twice the desired finished height, then folded and caught under on the inside to create a flat, clean finished edge.

Linked
A contrast trim is knitted separately and linked on after the garment is knitted. The stitches along the edge are picked up and the trim is attached by a few rows of knit, which form a seam inside the garment.

Picot
Decorative edge created by knitting regular pointelle holes along the middle of jersey trim, then folding the trim in half to form an undulating edge.

Flat strapping
Full needle rib trim, used as facing, in side slits or at necklines for a clean, finished look.

Single crochet
Stitches are picked up and crocheted to give a simple finished edge.

UNIT 14
developing a fabric story

Learning how to put together a fabric story is a true art, and an essential skill at the core of fashion design.

Like chefs who have perfected their technical skills, yet use their own personality and innovation to make the familiar extraordinary, fashion designers must also straddle two spectrums successfully to drive fashion forward, yet have the technical acumen to marry form with material so it appears effortless in execution.

Beginning with swatches for color and texture will provide you with initial information. However, advancing to larger swathes of fabric by unrolling yardage from the bolt and "mock draping" it on the human figure, to ensure that weight and drape form a happy marriage in your design, is an imperative practice before committing to each proposed swatch.

△ ▷ ▷ **Port of call**
A successful fabric story enhances the attitude, customer lifestyle, and price point of the collection. The plain weaves, varied weights, and sophisticated colors in cool cotton weaves support this bridge collection's attention to detail and mix-and-match separates.

The Five Rules When Designing with Fabric

Rule 1: The more complicated the design's construction, the plainer the fabric should be

Design that is intricate in seaming and construction often needs a fabric to support and not dominate the design focus. Either the fabric or the construction must be the focus, so they do not compete for attention. Imagine using a "nubby" wool bouclé for an organically seamed sheath dress. The sensitive line articulated through seaming wouldn't be visible because of the fabric's texture and density. Similarly, an intricately printed floral or beaded fabric carries enough design to be used in a simple, strapless evening column rather than a sculptural, elaborately draped silhouette.

Rule 2: Never force the fabric

Let the natural weight and drape of the fabric dictate the silhouette and type of garment. Design lacks conviction when the appropriate weights aren't married to the silhouettes successfully, resulting in a collection that lacks confidence and resolution. If the fabric is soft and drapey, avoid the temptation to tailor it. If the design is grand and sculptural, ensure the fabric can support the form rather than relying on complicated understructures.

Rule 3: Design to accentuate the natural characteristics of the fabric

All fabrics have a personality and "voice," and accentuating these through cut and silhouette gives substance to the design. Cut chiffons loose and billowy so they flaunt their weightlessness and transparency. Avoid pleating and draping bulky fabrics that are best shown in clean, tailored looks. Use charmeuse and similar shiny, fluid fabrics with draping and ruching, so that light is captured in the soft folds.

Rule 4: Vary fabric weights to create a dynamic collection

Creating a fabric story that incorporates various weights ensures that the silhouettes and construction effects in the collection will not be monotonous. The thrust of a collection can be focused on tailored shapes or softer, draped silhouettes, but employing a small element of the opposite helps accentuate your primary direction.

A frequent device employed by designers is to cut the same garment for a collection twice, using two different fabric weights that will give different personalities to the silhouette. For example, a trench coat might be cut in a stiff cotton canvas for daywear and in silk charmeuse for eveningwear, with modified proportion and detail. This not only gives the illusion that there are two designs because of the garment's reaction to the fabric it is cut in, but it also maintains design cohesion and is cost-effective.

Rule 5: Don't commit to a fabric until you've unrolled the bolt

A swatch that is 2 x 4 in. (5 x 10 cm) behaves differently when it is cut as a full garment. By unrolling the fabric bolt and draping a mock proportion to human scale, you gain a sense of drape, weight, appropriateness for the silhouette, and true scale of pattern/print. You may find that you need an alternate weight once a full yard or two is tested at full scale.

A SUCCESSFUL FABRIC STORY WILL:

• Support your concept and theme.

• Provide cohesion for the collection.

• Address your customer's needs, aesthetics, and lifestyle.

• Relate subtly to the previous and following deliveries for sales floor transitioning.

• Innovate fashion through application and/ or manufacturing techniques.

• Be consistent with the designer's identity and image.

• Address current trends while also providing an impetus for future ones.

• Contain a diverse range of fabric weights and textures.

• Address the intended season while simultaneously allowing for subtle shifts in temperature.

Fabric Quantities

The quantity of fabrics needed for a capsule collection of six to eight looks can rely on personal choice, customer needs, the type of collection developed, and the season addressed. However, by keeping a simple rubric in mind, you will have a working foundation for adjustment based on these criteria. For a six-to-eight sportswear capsule collection, for example, you should use the following quantities.

△ **Kaleidoscope kids** Abundant visual texture in pattern, detail, and trimmings give collections a playful attitude, particularly in childrenswear. When abundant patterns and prints are used, a harmonious color story is a must to maintain cohesion and clarity.

▷ **Speed racer** Bold colors, lightweight synthetic fabrics, and an emphasis on comfort give athletic-wear its signature look. Dynamic shapes of color move the viewer's eye and suggest high performance.

Two to three jacket/coat weights

Consider different weights for slight variations in the season's temperature, solids and patterns, natural and synthetics (if appropriate for your market), fabrics and skins (such as leather and suede). You will address different silhouettes and classification of these jackets/coats, so be sure your fabrics reflect this. For example, most fall/winter sportswear collections will give a tailored option, a shorter casual silhouette for weekends, and another that is either somewhere in between or a more fashion-forward item.

Two to three suiting weights

Not all designers feature traditional suits, but most collections feature their answer to this category's silhouette. From the traditional labels such as Burberry to the forward-thinking such as Comme des Garçons, this weight is used to cut jackets, trousers, and skirts, and is a core fabric within the group. Like the other categories, consider offering solids along with novelty choices such as stripes, checks, print, and textured fabrics, so your customer has options.

Two to three shirting/blouse weights

A highly versatile and varied weight, shirting/blouse weights are used in basic silhouettes to support a collection, as uniquely designed pieces that stand on their own without the need to layer, as color vehicles in solids and patterns, and even as larger silhouettes such as dresses. Solids and patterns, levels of sheer and opaque, matte and shine, crisp and fluid, flat weaves and textures can all contribute to a robust merchandising plan as well as diversity of silhouette.

Two to three knits

Every sportswear collection must contain an element of knitwear. Knitwear can cling to the body without darts or seams, can be tailored into suits, depending on the knit structure, and can be as sheer as chiffon or as dense as the heaviest coating. From cut-and-sew T-shirts to highly sculptural sweater knits that are works of art, knitwear's abilities are tremendous, particularly sweater knits where the fabric is developed for the desired pattern shape and form.

Consider the combination of two and one when composing your knit quantities; two cut-and-sew options with one sweater knit, or one cut-and-sew and two sweater knits. Diverse weights will ensure silhouettes are varied and merchandising is resolved, along with solids and patterns, textures, and varied fiber contents.

Two to three novelties

Novelties add surprise and drama to your collection. They are often used in small amounts to support core fabrics and items. Novelty weaves, textures, patterns, and fabric techniques can all support layered looks as items that are not core to the group and may even be used in larger silhouettes in small quantities. Consider how a lace camisole or metallic brocade can add to a capsule collection through color or texture. How could a fabric technique, such as embroidery, relate to the core fabrics and colors to help break up the generality of the group and convey a concept or inspiration?

UNIT 15
silhouette

A common device employed by designers when developing a collection is silhouette repetition.

As a collection is presented, a repeated contour of the figure is used in a similar manner in order to communicate the collection's emphasis. The interpretation of this silhouette will vary through shape, fabric weight, placement on the figure, and proportion, but having a defined silhouette gives the collection a sense of cohesion.

Fashion history has frequently seen silhouettes that were in contrast to those preceding them. The sweeping, flared skirts and tailored jackets of Dior's "New Look" emphasized an extreme wasp waist and followed the slimmer silhouettes designed during World War II when fabric restrictions were enforced. The elongated, drop-waist silhouette of the 1920s used vertical parallel lines to produce an androgynous, rectangular silhouette that negated the body underneath and served as a reaction to the corseted hourglass waists of the turn of the century. More recently, the soft, untailored jacket shoulders of the 1990s were in contrast to the severe, padded power-suit shoulders of the 1980s.

△ **Forever Dior** Often working from a silhouette that led to collections named "H-Line," "Y-Line," "Tulip," and "Figure 8," the "A-Line" collection of spring 1955 was defined by its triangular silhouette.

PRACTICAL CONSIDERATIONS

Consider how to vary the silhouette's placement, proportion, and fabric in each look so that the articulation varies. The A-line silhouettes of a three-quarter coat cut in a stiff cotton canvas, a lightweight, cashmere knit tunic, and a charmeuse, bias-cut, flared skirt are equally effective in communicating a silhouette focus. The fabric drape and texture, garment proportion, and color will convey different feelings that will vary the interpretation of the A-line silhouette while keeping the collection's emphasis united.

△ **Symphony in A-major** Beethoven's music and period menswear inspired this collection's A-line silhouette and ruffle detail. By varying proportions and fabric weights, a silhouette will change as a collection develops, so avoiding monotony and repetition.

◁ **Long and lean** The vertical silhouette of tailored sportswear looks neat and professional. To convey a "cool, calm, and collected" aesthetic, avoid segmenting the body in multiple proportions, colors, and textures.

◁◁ **Buddha's circle** Inspired by ancient Tibetan art, the cocoon silhouette of this collection displays varying degrees of design intensity. Designers filter a pure silhouette concept from its most extreme to one that is suggested to create engaging levels in the intensity of the design.

UNIT 16
the basics of creating a collection

The success of a collection is determined by how well defined the message is that the designer wishes to communicate.

The intensity of the defining criteria—motif, color, fabric, and specificity of customer identity—must vary, so there will be areas where an inspiration may appear as literal manifestations of the theme as well as garment shapes and details that convey a broader context.

Given the quantity of looks a designer may present at a fashion show, it is not surprising that the methods for unifying an underlying theme can be expansive. By using various degrees of inspiration representation, designers not only keep an audience engaged during a presentation, but also cast their net to a broad target market while simultaneously offering their core customers "one-stop shopping." A customer may wish to wear a very fashion-forward look one day, and opt for a more familiar silhouette that is less extreme (and possibly more comfortable) another.

The Successful Collection

The collection advances fashion forward

This is a goal that all designers reach for each season. Although an inspiration may come from the past, fashion must always look forward and strive to innovate and recontextualize the existing market. By advancing in new technologies, interpretations, sustainable methods, purposes, and even by creating new consumer groups, designers drive our culture forward and charter new pathways that innovate the industry as a whole.

The collection is unique to the designer's "thumbprint"

An original and easily identifiable product maintains a loyal customer base while also garnering excellent brand recognition. Collections shown during a city's fashion week frequently blur together, lack originality in vision, and seem homogenized; remaining unique among a sea of other designers gives integrity and identity to the label.

◁ △ **Visionary** A designer's message must always remain pure and focused; the severe graphic colors and silhouettes displayed here are amplified by both stiff fabrics and accessories.

Varying the intensity of the concept

By offering a range of looks that is literal to your inspiration and concept, along with filtered, "watered-down" versions, designers satisfy their customers' needs and shifting moods. Variation keeps an audience engaged during a runway show and allows retailers to buy a collection that caters to their clientele's aesthetic.

Merchandising addresses a range of occasions

Designers must provide their customers with one-stop shopping in each collection. By merchandising their items and offering a full wardrobe that ranges from day to night and includes tailored looks along with softer looks, designers are ensuring that they meet their customers' needs for various occasions and moods.

In a typical runway show, the presentation order begins with tailored looks that are vertical in silhouette, followed by the "item-driven" sportswear segment, with more complex color, texture, and silhouette relationships, and ends with the cocktail and evening options.

When building a collection, consider offering silhouettes that convey a more extreme version of your concept along with those that merely suggest it in varied degrees of intensity.

Order of presentation builds momentum and provides narration

An essential element in any runway show and presentation is the order in which a theme is presented. For some designers, defined color palettes within individual groups give small, digestible capsules in the whole show's context. Other designers build a narrative in their show that begins with fairly conventional silhouettes and gradually crescendos into a fantasy world of extremities, as is often seen with Alexander McQueen. Yet another device is to have these extreme silhouettes and garments filtered throughout a collection, where they serve as a reminder of the theme/concept and, in turn, reinforce the collection's direction among the more generalized looks. Whichever device is used, it is important to retain an element of surprise and one of cohesion through the various design foci already discussed.

▽ **Crescendo** The order of presentation is well thought out in this day-to-night group. Vertical silhouettes "bookend" the capsule, central looks focus on fabric and motif juxtapositions, and accent color is laid out for maximum effect.

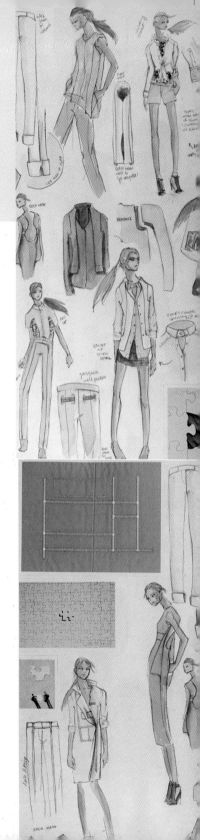

CHAPTER 3

developing your design process

During the development of a collection, designers follow a sequenced chain of creative processes that builds upon each preceding link. By developing a collection's narration in consecutive steps, the process remains fluid, well investigated, and thorough. While working through these steps of inspiration, conception, research accumulation, mood-board creation, fabric selection, the croquis process, and final editing, designers remain focused and methodical. Following this process also gives designers the chance to garner feedback from colleagues and select magazine editors and retailers before they advance to the next, more committed level in building their collection.

This section gives a commonly used "road map" for working through the creative process. Following this will allow you to conceptualize, develop, and refine each area of your work, from the inception of an inspiration, through the design process, and on to the final edits where a merchandising plan is followed. This order for building a collection also provides an accurate assimilation in the professional design room, where fabric yardages must be ordered far in advance, so that they may arrive when the looks have been selected and are ready for prototyping.

▷ **Step by step** Building the design in stages is critical when forming collections, whether there are six looks or sixty. Design specificity in addition to a collection's coalescence must be considered equally when designing a seasonal collection.

An illustrated dictionary in this section provides basic references to fundamental garment details and classic silhouettes that you can use when developing ideas. By acquiring a basic working knowledge of construction details, the appropriate methods may be selected to best suit fabric choice, the collection's concept, and the market.

Similarly, having knowledge of iconic silhouettes will help in contextualizing a collection thematically, and may even serve as a foundation for challenging preconceived notions of what a garment's category and meaning are.

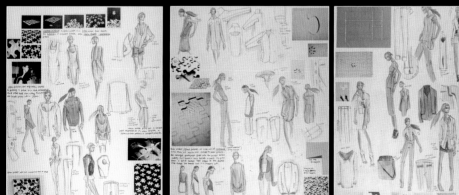

△ **All in good order** The visual connection of motif between looks allows the garments to build upon one another as they are presented. Opening looks must serve as a subtle introduction, and closing looks can give the exclamation point to the finale.

UNIT 17

mood boards

Like an overture before a film begins, a mood board signals what is to come through mood, color, customer, detail, and aesthetic.

Mood boards are used to introduce a group in a portfolio or during a briefing meeting attended by design room staff at the beginning of a collection's development. The board provides the viewer with a "space to inhabit" when viewing the work, and can give a design room team the foundations for researching material and fabric.

The success of a mood board relies heavily on image editing and artistic expression that complements the intended mood and aura for the preconceived collection. What is not shown is just as important as what is. Image scale, placement, manipulation via the computer or other device, choice of papers, and types of images chosen must all carry intention and purpose while also communicating a clear direction to both the designer and the "fresh eye."

A successful mood board gives viewers a tease to the collection and introduces what will follow. The board may even serve as a tease to the general public, including editors and retailers, as designers discuss their intended direction for the season during preview meetings and obtain feedback before advancing.

△▽ **Motif and meaning** Inspired by the abuse of horses used in nineteenth-century factories, this collection makes a commentary about man's mistreatment of animals. Horse bridle and harness shapes create a collection that ends on an ethereal note.

◁ **Clean sweep** When finalizing a fabric board, designers often organize swatches in the order in which they will transition during the presentation. This allows them to check issues of color rhythm as well as the adequacy of the merchandising.

PRACTICAL CONSIDERATIONS

When composing a mood board, start by analyzing what the general arc and message of the collection is and how your board can elicit the same emotions you want the audience to feel when they view your collection. Research that offers qualitative and quantitative material for design via color, silhouette, period detail, styling, textures, fabric treatments, and other design-centric specificities should be reviewed and edited down to the images that offer a "gesture" of the concepts that will inhabit the collection.

◁ **Thrown a curve** Considering how line has been used in art and architecture through two- and three-dimensional means led this designer to reference the apple peel, which can be viewed in both dimensions.

▽ **Practicing principles** Inspired by an apple peel and the act of its removal, these sketches focus on the relationships and proportions of line, and how line remnants can create new shapes, textures, and varieties of motif development.

UNIT 18
garment construction

Having a comprehensive vocabulary of garment detail and classic silhouettes provides you with a working knowledge of the tools you will need while designing.

Familiarity of garment construction will also increase your ability to contextualize a collection in theme and inspiration. Iconic garments and details, such as the safari jacket or the sailor collar, can reference a theme the designer has utilized for updating the form and context, and may even offer conceptual narration.

On the following pages, there are some well-known terms associated with garment detail and iconic silhouettes. By adjusting proportion, fabric, color, and even category, a collection can become innovative and advance fashion in unseen ways. How could a leather biker jacket that is constructed in transparent chiffon alter its purpose and category? How could denim be used in eveningwear silhouettes to deconstruct its utilitarian origins? How could knitwear be utilized in a silhouette commonly executed in a woven fabric, such as a trench coat, to alter the wearer's experience?

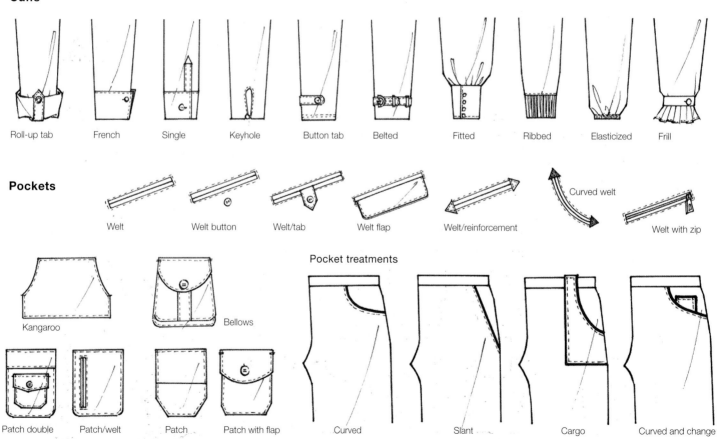

Cuffs

Roll-up tab   French   Single   Keyhole   Button tab   Belted   Fitted   Ribbed   Elasticized   Frill

Pockets

Welt   Welt button   Welt/tab   Welt flap   Welt/reinforcement   Curved welt   Welt with zip

Kangaroo   Bellows

Patch double   Patch/welt   Patch   Patch with flap

Pocket treatments

Curved   Slant   Cargo   Curved and change

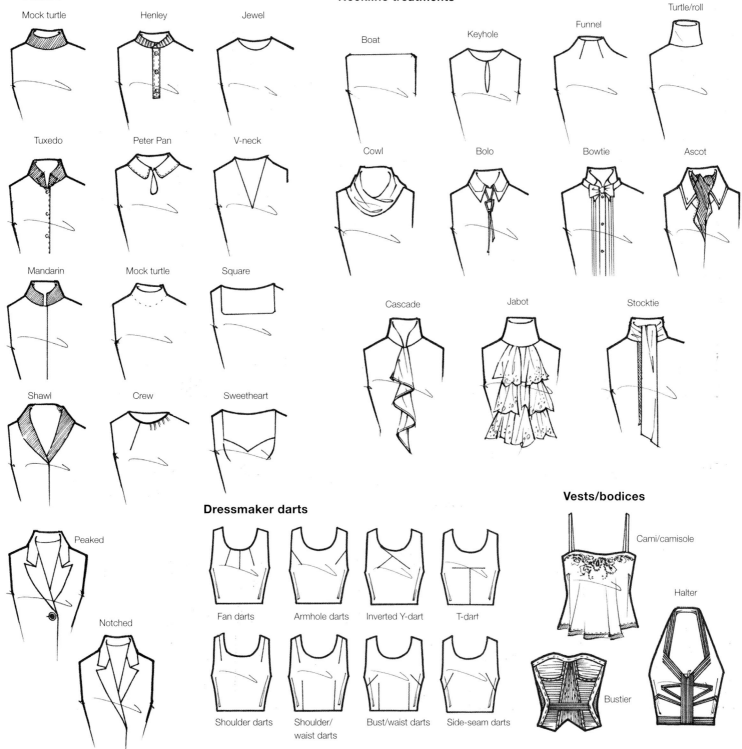

Collars

Mock turtle

Henley

Jewel

Tuxedo

Peter Pan

V-neck

Mandarin

Mock turtle

Square

Shawl

Crew

Sweetheart

Peaked

Notched

Neckline treatments

Boat

Keyhole

Funnel

Turtle/roll

Cowl

Bolo

Bowtie

Ascot

Cascade

Jabot

Stocktie

Dressmaker darts

Fan darts

Armhole darts

Inverted Y-dart

T-dart

Shoulder darts

Shoulder/ waist darts

Bust/waist darts

Side-seam darts

Vests/bodices

Cami/camisole

Halter

Bustier

Tops and details

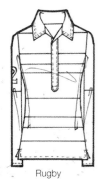
Rugby

Polo

Tee

Camp

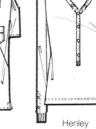
Henley

Epaulet

Close-up of epaulet

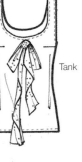
Tank

Vest

Weskit

Anatomy of a shirt

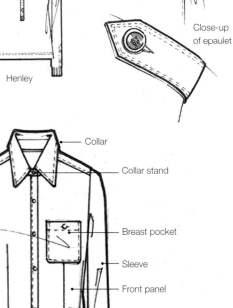

Collar

Yoke

Collar stand

Breast pocket

Sleeve

Front panel

Button band plackett

Cuff

Blouses and shirts

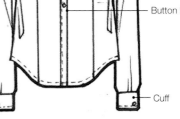

Shell tank

Western

Bowling

Sailor/midday

Peasant/gypsy

Poet/artist's smock

Tuxedo formal

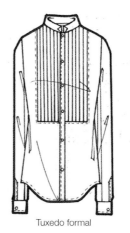

Coats and outerwear

Cocoon

Peacoat

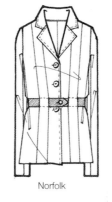

Balmacaan

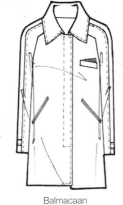

Norfolk

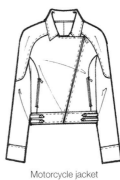

Motorcycle jacket

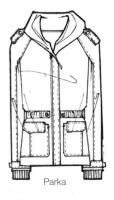

Parka

Trench coat

Mackintosh

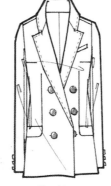

Chesterfield

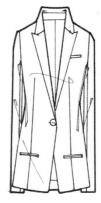

Kent blazer

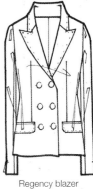

Traditional blazer

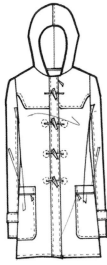

Regency blazer

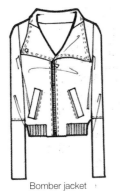

Duffel coat

Bomber jacket

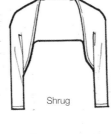

Shrug

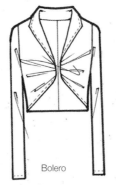

Bolero

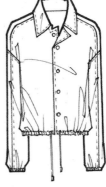

Windbreaker

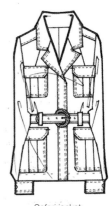

Safari jacket

Skirts

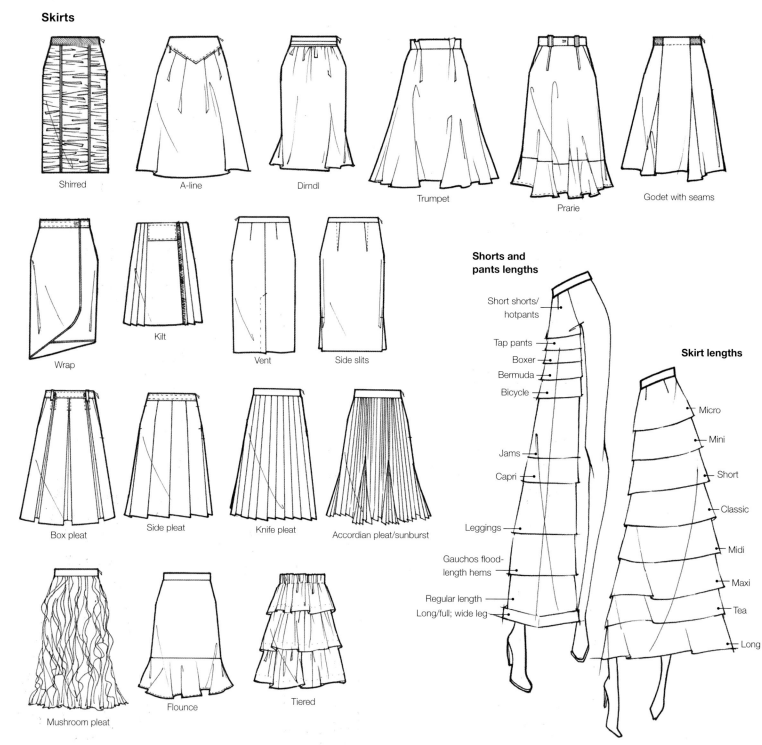

Shirred

A-line

Dirndl

Trumpet

Prarie

Godet with seams

Wrap

Kilt

Vent

Side slits

Shorts and pants lengths

Short shorts/ hotpants

Tap pants

Boxer

Bermuda

Bicycle

Jams

Capri

Leggings

Gauchos flood-length hems

Regular length

Long/full; wide leg

Skirt lengths

Micro

Mini

Short

Classic

Midi

Maxi

Tea

Long

Box pleat

Side pleat

Knife pleat

Accordian pleat/sunburst

Mushroom pleat

Flounce

Tiered

Dresses

Halter

Wrap

Trapeze

Slip

Empire waist

Pouf

Sheath

Blouson

Cheongsam

Shirt dress

Halter

UNIT 19

croquis books

Croquis books involve every skill-based and conceptual application of fashion design we have discussed so far.

The croquis process is an especially important one for a fashion designer to master. The croquis book is a creative space that allows designers to experiment, propose concepts, clarify construction, communicate mood, refine ideas, make mistakes, and ultimately create a successful collection. In short, a croquis book is a visual (and sometimes textural) documentary of how a collection is developed.

PRACTICAL CONSIDERATIONS

All designers approach the process with their own unique style. It is essential when developing ideas to find a system that works most effectively for you—one that does not inhibit creative development and allows you to produce well-resolved work. The size of the book, quality of paper, materials used for illustration, composition of the page, and methods for building the work are all areas that must be experimented with when attempting to find which systems suit a particular designer.

▽ **Design intention** Color matching, clean lines, and accurate proportion all contribute to information being accurately communicated.

CONSIDER THE FOLLOWING CRITERIA WHEN EXPERIMENTING WITH DIFFERENT PROCESSES FOR CROQUIS DEVELOPMENT:

Book size

Use a size that feels most manageable and one that allows you to compose the page with sufficiently scaled figures in well-conceived compositions. It is essential in the design process to see how a collection progresses, as opposed to composing pages with isolated figures that prevent viewers from seeing the design evolution. A size that works very well is 11 x 14 in. (28 x 35.5 cm). It will also need to contain paper that handles wet and dry media well.

Design representation

Communicating design effectively and in a manner that engages your viewer relies heavily upon several factors. The scale in which you draw is essential, because to draw an accurate proportion of a pocket shape or collar angle in a scale that is too small will undermine the specificity and design intention you may have.

Equally important is how the design is developed and composed on the page. Working on a figure for garment proportion and silhouette, design can gain clarity and intention through the use of garment flats and blown-up detail shots for specifics such as finishing details. When working in a croquis book, it is essential to maintain clarity in the design's visual communication so that your viewer may understand your process best, and so that the designer may be best informed when progressing.

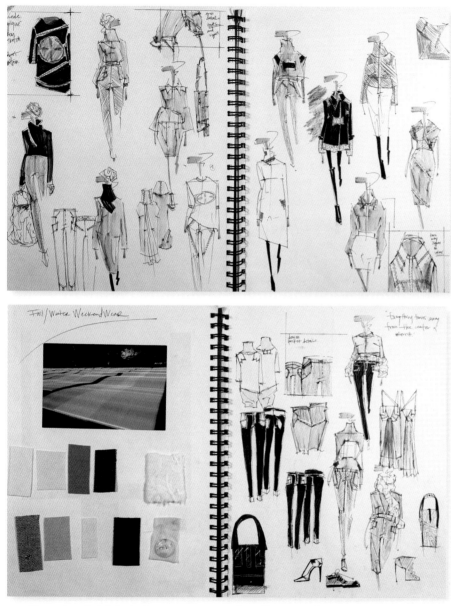

△△ **Character sketch** Illustration style, figure layout, use of flats with detail shots, drawing medium, and text all support a designer's aesthetic and customer. Viewing diverse approaches to professional fashion illustration can provide inspiration for finding a successful method.

△ **Installing order** Organizing each group in the same sequence gives viewers a prescribed framework upon which to focus on design development. Research, swatches, and croquis support each other in a well-told narrative.

METHODOLOGIES FOR THE DESIGN PROCESS

For many designers, simultaneously tackling the design process, page composition, and illustration accuracy in the croquis is overwhelming. To mitigate this, divide the process into two steps.

• Strategically compose the pages by gesturing figures in pencil and allowing blank spaces beside them for detail shots and garment flats; a basic figure with an S-curve and high hip is all that is needed. Consider taking a break after five to six pages have been laid out. This will allow you to shift gears successfully before you begin the creative process of design, when you will immerse yourself in the collection's mood and concepts.

• Begin the design process in a manner that suits you. For some designers, working in an organized and sequenced left-to-right manner allows them to see the design progression most clearly. Other designers prefer to design on the gestured figures first, and will then go back to the open spaces for designing garment flats with greater specificity that are based on the figure's designs. Designers who find it difficult to focus on a specific aspect of the collection, and how it must be evolved gradually, may design and/or draw garment flats that do not relate and then return to visually fill in the gaps with a more sequenced and strategic use of motif, color, and fabric based on the initially drawn, isolated looks.

Whichever process is selected, a croquis book must always supply the viewer with a visual documentation of the design process, illustrate how a theme was translated into a collection, communicate design and conceptual ideas clearly, and offer versions of the designs and motifs used in the collection to provide options when merchandising.

▽ **Extrapolating elements** Dissecting elements from the various sources of inspiration for color, print, fabric, and motif, all comes from well-planned initial research. If you struggle for criteria to design with, reconsider the validity of your inspiration base.

▷ **Information highway** This high level of blouse development demonstrates how the personality of a garment can change based on the slightest alteration. The seaming shown for a chiffon blouse all results in a similar silhouette, yet provides highly individual feelings.

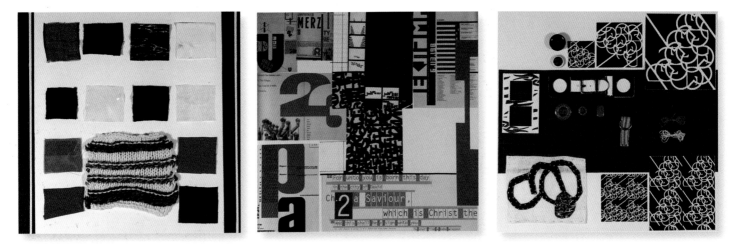

THE HALLMARKS OF A SUCCESSFUL CROQUIS BOOK

Organized framework

By maintaining a similar presentation layout for all groups within the croquis book, the clothing becomes easier to focus on. Each group's order should consist of inspiration pages, fabric swatches, forty to fifty croquis per group, an accessories page, and the six to eight edits that will make up the group. By introducing the inspiration and fabrics first, your viewer has a context for the colors, fabrics, motifs, silhouettes, and mood of the collection.

Clarity of communication

The use of notes, well-rendered fabrics, accurately matched colors to fabric swatches, a drawing scale that is large enough to precisely depict design intention, and a well-composed page all allow your viewer to understand the design development, while also ensuring that the design intentions and specificities are understood correctly.

Depth of context in design

A well-designed group contains depth and levels of context as it relates to the inspiration. Consider beginning the group with the more literal representations or the extreme aspects of the collection and then adapt the collection as it progresses. How can the literal aspects that have been extrapolated from the research, including silhouette, fabric treatment, color relationships, and garment construction, be altered from their purest form into a broader context that still relates to the inspiration and mood?

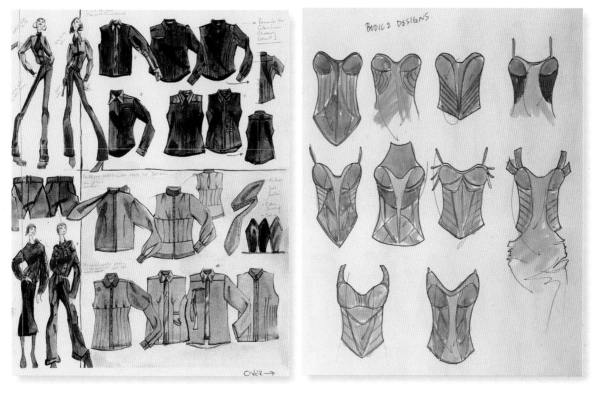

BODICE DESIGNS.

OVER→

◁ **Notes on a theme**
It is essential to experiment with proportions, color relationships, details, and placements of these elements when designing. By providing different versions, designers are sure to find the best solution and to move forward with their ideas.

Variety and options offered

A primary purpose for using a croquis book is to allow the designer to expand upon initial speculations of design, and to investigate options through versions of design. By altering a garment's proportion and details, considering new ways to fabricate and coordinate the same silhouette, finding various approaches for styling the collection, and appropriating a detail and/or motif to other items for cohesion, the designer creates options for editing a well-resolved collection.

Strategic merchandising

The quantity of fabrics and the silhouettes they are appropriated to, the options given for a variety of occasions and subtle changes in the season's temperature, and a diversity of design intensities that ranges from the most literal to the more filtered, all contribute to providing your targeted audience with a well-formulated collection. By offering a range to your audience, retailers are able to buy selected pieces from the collection to best suit their customers.

Identity

One of the most important aspects of being a designer is to convey a unique and defined personality and identity through the croquis book, which can give conviction to the work. Consider how the style of figures drawn can convey the customer best. How can the choice of illustration medium, figure styling, layout and composition, use and style of text, methods for adhering images and swatches, and various other elements of art direction create a focused aesthetic and identity?

Your croquis book is like the design of a retail store. It should support the clothing's aesthetic but not dominate the collection, which must always remain the focus.

UNIT 20
editing and merchandising

A primary component of designers' success is their ability to edit croquis sketches into a well-formulated, well-merchandised collection.

Maximizing a collection's purpose, artistically and economically, relies on knowing the customer, having a keen perception of the direction in which fashion is advancing, maintaining an informed relationship with retailers and their clientele, and creating a strategic plan for how your label's image will be developed for a consumer audience.

Something for Everyone and Every Occasion

For some designers, the collection produced for the runway serves to generate media "buzz," and a second collection is adapted from these showpieces and produced for retail. For other design houses, particularly those who do not produce runway shows, the merchandising formula is a strictly adhered-to recipe that dictates when deliveries are placed on the retail selling floor and the ratio of garment types in the collection.

The core element of merchandising centers upon the idea of offering your customer "one-stop shopping." A collection must offer all components, and with varying degrees of design intensity and inspiration interpretation. Although the collection must be united in mood, fabric selection, and price point, offering a more "familiar" silhouette of a jacket in addition to one that is more "forward" will not only entice two types of customer, but will also provide your core customer with an essential silhouette that serves two different occasions or moods.

▷ **Highs and lows** A successfully merchandised collection like this one gives the customer options of silhouette, fabric, extremities of design, and range of price points within its category.

Example of a Merchandising Formula

Although the merchandising formula may vary based on such criteria as season and customer, a typical six-look collection could consist of the following offerings:

Three outerwear options

Offerings should include a tailored option, a shorter option, and a novelty version. An example for a fall/winter collection would be a three-quarter-length, camel-hair coat for professional situations, a hip-length peacoat cut in a medium-weight wool felt with windowpane pattern for less severe temperatures, and a cashmere-lined, nylon-hooded, zip-front jacket for casual wear.

Two to three jackets

Although not all designers will offer the traditional tailored jacket, this category must be addressed primarily through fabric weights. Fabrics may include wools, cottons, leather and suede, nylons, and knits that have little "give" and are thus able to be tailored. Styles could include a pant suit for professional occasions, a less constructed soft-shoulder jacket in a pattern or print, a more informal and casual silhouette in leather that could also serve as outerwear, or a cropped style in a metallic fabric.

Two to three woven shirts/blouses

A simple, classic silhouette can serve as a piece to layer items on top of; more intricately designed silhouettes stand on their own.

Some designers offer a range of designs and fabrics, but others provide their customer with a minimal selection because of the label's aesthetic. A capsule collection could consist of a classic, crisp, white cotton shirt as a layering item, a multicolor printed blouse in silk georgette, and a bias-cut, charmeuse, draped halter top.

Two to three knits

Similar to the shirt/blouse category, knitwear can provide options for layering, or encompass uniquely designed pieces that make strong statements on their own. It is essential when merchandising knitwear to offer dramatically different weights within the group, so that the items offered don't appear redundant to your customer. A cut-and-sew jersey in a long-sleeved T-shirt silhouette, a fine-gauge cashmere, sweater-knit cardigan with architectural rib-knit detail, a medium-gauge cotton sweater with pattern or graphic, a suede cord that is knitted to provide an element of texture, and a sculptural, chunky wool sweater used as a statement piece all demonstrate the diverse "experiences" and purposes of knitwear for the customer.

Two to three pants

From wide and slim leg, cuffed and pegged hems, pleated and flat-front waistlines, tailored trousers to drawstring-waist track pants, and even knit leggings, pant silhouettes must offer the customer various shapes, details, and fabrics. From a more tailored option that has a wide leg and lots of swing, to a crisp stovepipe leg that elongates the figure, to a novelty fabric, such as nylon or charmeuse that captures light and can address another type of category within the capsule because of its versatility, care must be given in offering versatility of silhouette and how fabric addresses usage. This category also includes shorts for spring/summer collections.

Two to three skirts

Similar to pant merchandising, skirts must adhere closely to the group's category, mood, and customer needs while also offering varying silhouettes, fabric weights, and levels of design detail. From a simple A-line skirt cut in the same fabric as a tailored jacket, through a nylon skirt with zipper and topstitching detail, to a bias-cut, charmeuse, knee-length, printed silhouette that could go from day to night as a slightly dressier option, a capsule collection must offer skirts that maintain versatility in usage and in how they are coordinated with other items.

One to two dresses

The quantity and complexity of dresses offered can range from a simple, straight sheath dress that provides color flow, support, or both, to a more designed piece that is layered on top, from a sculpturally draped column in matte jersey that conveys a more formal presence, to a detailed summer dress in cotton voile. Consider how a dress can serve as its own focus through the use of design intensity or fabric without the need to layer, or as a simpler silhouette that provides support to an item that is placed on top of it through the use of a color or design motif that relates to the collection in a secondary or tertiary manner.

The Edit Page

It is essential, after the croquis stage, to compose an edit page, where the final looks are shown together in the order in which they will be presented. An edit page allows the designer to make subtle changes in the group's design so that the sum of the whole is successfully resolved before advancing to muslin prototypes. By viewing the looks together, the collection can be reevaluated in terms of color flow, texture placement, fabric, motif manipulation, silhouette cohesion, and design intensity. For traditional sportswear collections, it is imperative to analyze how items will coordinate with one another by mixing and matching them so that the customer has a full range of options based on how they may wish to style the pieces.

△ **Weekend equestrian**
The romance and history of equestrian sports are captured in this contemporary collection that has a denim, leather, and knitwear focus. Fabrics selected must all reflect the specific price point within the group for merchandising costs.

◁ **Cruising**
Merchandising for specific categories is often dictated by a narrative of the customer's lifestyle. The soft fabrics and relaxed silhouettes reflect the environment of a cruise collection inspired by travels on the Aegean Sea.

◁ **Out to play** Motif and dynamic, graphic textures keep this boyswear group in playful spirits. Allowing for shifts in climate, events, and types of detailing in a group ensures that the collection will appeal to a broad audience.

◁ **Same palette, different looks** Brown, white, and shades in between keep this collection focused, while the artistic fabric treatments and construction details prevent monotony. When a color palette is minimal, garment detail, silhouettes, and fabrics must vary greatly within the collection.

assignments

As a developing professional it is essential that you learn various methodologies for approaching the fashion design process. By investigating various types of research foundations, conceptual applications, and ways in which to build a successful collection, designers not only learn which methods are most successful for them, but also challenge and exercise their creative muscle by stepping out of their "comfort zones" and using unexplored and unfamiliar design processes.

This chapter provides individual exercises based on some of the most frequently used concepts for developing collections. Although the design process may vary within each framework, the outcomes and how a collection's success is assessed are universal. From the historical narratives frequently orchestrated by John Galliano and Alexander McQueen, to the architectural and clean lines conceived by Narciso Rodriguez and Isabel Toledo, and the conceptually charged and forward-thinking ideas of Rei Kawakubo at Comme des Garçons and Hussein Chalayan, designers solidify their identities each season and refine their personal artistic developments, all while innovating the current fashion industry.

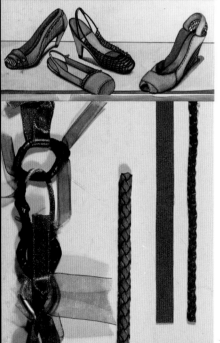

◁ **Trims and textures** Designing with specificity gives a collection its indelible thumbprint. How a designer incorporates design details often provides the hallmarks for a collection and the brand's image.

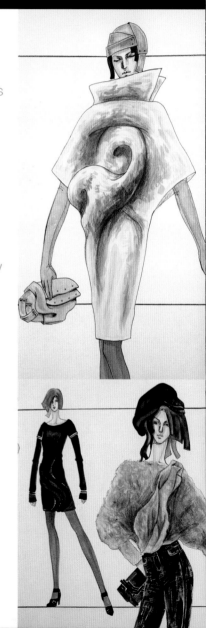

IT IS IMPORTANT WHILE DEVELOPING AS A PROFESSIONAL TO KEEP THE FOLLOWING CRITERIA IN MIND:

....

- Having a focused point of view and bringing a new "plot" to the table is essential. Sometimes it isn't the design that's necessarily new, but how it's framed.

- Adaptability to all that is changing in the world is vital, whether it is technology, socio-political situations, cultural shifts, consumer behaviors, etc. Fashion designers strive to know what consumers will want a year or more from now.

- The industry demands well-rounded designers who can create something that is relevant to today and aesthetically in demand, but also designers who understand the lifestyle and motivations of their consumers.

- Designers must have content and context in their work, and it must always remain relevant to today's world through historical, cultural, societal, political, and economic observations.

- Knowing the current market, how to operate and create within boundaries, and developing a basic business acumen allows professionals to create a more marketable point of view.

- Developing designers must always exercise their creative muscle by exploring the different methods used when creating collections, including: the types of inspirations, the materials used, contexts and usage, and customer parameters and price points.

- Necessary skill building is key to design knowledge, ensuring that a designer's technical "vocabulary" is broad; this allows designers to solve problems with whichever techniques will be most successful.

- Designers understand that design is, on some levels, problem solving.

- Designers today are required to wear a staggering array of hats, all at an equal level. Education must produce complete designers, not just illustrators, seamstresses, digital designers, or, for that matter, "conceptualists."

▽ **Designer levels**
Collections must always contain varieties of detail and silhouette complexity. Offering simplified and classic designs alongside the more detailed and sculptural ensures your customers' needs are fully addressed.

Assignment 1
shopping reports

Visiting a store to see collections and current trends is one of the best ways to be well informed. This assignment guides you through the important elements you should have in mind as you look around.

■ AIMS

- Analyze collections sold and the retail store experience
- Understand how the environment underscores the designer's aspirational world and aesthetic identity
- Note how environment and experience give a strong foundation for clothing

Whether you are a student or a professional designer, shopping reports will keep you up-to-date with market trends and inform you of garment construction, finishing techniques, fabrics, color stories, merchandising, what is selling at retail, what is on the sales rack, and what customers are responding to most. Visiting a boutique will also show you how the retail experience and environment communicate and synthesize the designer's vision and clothing.

THE BIG PLAYERS

When you visit larger stores, such as Saks Fifth Avenue, Barneys, or Bloomingdale's, notice which designers are shown alongside each other. They tend to have similar audiences and aesthetics, so that customers can access brands with comparable styles, price points, and even garment fits most easily.

◁▷ **Customer frameworks**
Designers clearly define their customer so collections remain focused and well edited. The graphic shapes and neutral tones of this grouping suggest a customer who appreciates innovative and bold architectural construction.

■ METHOD

Visit stores, noting your impressions of the following categories:

The clothes

- Identify the market: designer/bridge/moderate/budget?
- What is the color story?
- List the fabrics used: fiber content and specific fabric names.
- Note the garment details: beading/fabric prints/contrast stitching/pleating/washings/logo buttons/logo zippers/logo rivets/patch pockets/cargo pockets. Consider their placement, imagery, size, shape, and materials used.
- Think about the merchandising of garments: Are there more skirts than pants?
- How many pieces of a given style are on a rack?
- Note the size range available (XS/S/M or 2/4/6 or 36/38/40).
- Identify the garment fit.
- What is the inspiration and overall statement of the collection?
- What appears to be the must-have item or items being pushed for the season?
- What is your response to the clothes?
- Include detailed drawings of some garments.

◁ △ **Construction via concept**
The "Siamese twin" effect of this updated shirt and trench coat share the concept of conjoined garments in different manners to create a well-conceptualized collection.

The retail experience

- Consider the store layout/atmosphere: lighting, music, scent, color scheme.
- Does the store layout complement the collection? Why or why not?
- Who is the customer: age, occupation, lifestyle, and so on?
- Where does the individual wear the clothes?
- Which other designers have retail spaces adjacent to the boutique or floor space? Are they similar? How and why?
- What is the location of the store and what does this communicate about the customer and aesthetic?
- Which stores are in proximity? Do they share a similar price point and customer audience?
- What kind of experience does the architect give the customer? How do you feel within the store? How do these aspects relate to the customer and their choices for fashion?

◁ **Advancing the ordinary**
The traditional menswear shirt is rethought through construction for a bold interpretation. How familiar or innovative a silhouette is speaks to customer lifestyle and product usage.

Assignment 2

architecture

Architecture and fashion design remain synonymous in their need to address the human condition and their reliance on ergonomics. This assignment guides you through using an architectural style as inspiration for design.

△ **Shapes to come**
Louis Khan's iconic use of the triangle and circle (above, right) inspires this eveningwear collection. Triangular pleating and silhouettes combine with full circular hemlines and accessory details in varying fabrics and treatments.

From the opulent Italian baroque period, to the ordered symmetry of the Georgian period, and the rigid lines and geometry favored by Mies van der Rohe, the concepts elicited by architecture are as varied as the fashion aesthetics that have been created for today's consumer. In a similar way to all aspects of design, architecture comments on the shifts that have occurred in society. For example, the Arts and Crafts movement was a reaction to the dominant industrialization of design and strove to create design that reflected a handcrafted look. For these reasons, architecture provides a rich source of design inspiration.

■ AIMS

- Learn how architecture and design reflect personality and associations
- Research a specific period/structure
- Extrapolate visual material and concepts

TIMELINE OF ARCHITECTURAL STYLES

Classical (400 BCE–)
Iconic in ancient Greece and Rome, the style followed a strict set of rules and proportions still used today. Features: bold and simple moldings, columned colonnades, heavy cornices, symmetrical shapes, pediment gables. Example: Parthenon, Athens.

Gothic (1100 to mid-1400s)
Evolved from Romanesque and the arches of Moorish architecture seen in Spain. Features: pointed arches, ribbed vaulting, flying buttresses, stained-glass windows, gargoyles. Examples: Chartres Cathedral, near Paris; Notre Dame Cathedral, Paris.

Renaissance (1400 to 1600)
Simplification of classical architecture. Features: symmetry, classical columns,

Consider the following framework when analyzing your chosen inspiration, applying the questions to your collection as it is developed.

- How are form, color, and texture used? How do these accentuate the feelings of the architect's design and message? How do they define the particular period?

- How do you feel emotionally when you move through the space? How does this reflect on the environment's purpose?

- How is light used or omitted? How can this inform textile selection or motif?

- How does the structure's form relate to its surroundings? Do the surroundings support the structure and allow it to blend in, or is the building juxtaposed with its environment?

- What is the historical context of the work and how can this inform a design concept? What societal forces occurred during its inception?

- What are the primary concepts the architect worked with? How does the design exhibit those concepts? How can fashion design exhibit the same concepts?

- Examining the breadth of the architect's work, how did his or her style evolve and why?

- Has your researched structure physically evolved over time? What were the reasons for these changes and do these make a commentary on the societal framework that could inform your concept?

- Examining the dominant styles that preceded and followed your investigated period, how could the impetus for such changes inform how a collection might evolve through its presentation?

---

triangular pediments, proportion and line, rounded arches, domes. Examples: Villa La Rotunda, near Vicenza; Saint Peter's Basilica, Vatican City.

Baroque (1600 to early 1800s)
Italian, French, English, and Spanish colonial. Features: extravagant, highly complicated decoration. Examples: churches commissioned by Catholic popes; Palace of Versailles, Paris.

Rocco (mid-1600s to end of the 1700s)
Similar to baroque, but lighter, softer, and more graceful. Features: shell and plant motifs, pastel colors. Example: Hermitage Winter Palace, Saint Petersburg.

Georgian (1700 to 1800)
Stately and highly symmetrical. Features: decorative crown over the front door, five windows across the front, flattened columns on each side of the door. Example: Royal Crescent, Bath, UK.

Federalist (late 1700s to mid-1800s)
Adapted from British Georgian style: circular or elliptical rooms, semicircular fanlights above doors, low-pitched roofs with balustrades, circular or elliptical windows, shutters, narrow side windows flanking the doorway. Example: Julia Row, New Orleans.

Greek revival (mid-1800s)
First appropriated to public buildings and later to homes for the affluent. Features: based on classical. Example: Leo von Klenze's Walhalla, Bavaria.

Victorian (mid-1800s to 1900)
Hybridization of various styles, diverse in representation. Features: lacy "gingerbread" trim, towers, wraparound porches, fanciful details, mansard roofs, brackets under eves. Example: Manchester Town Hall, UK.

Arts and Crafts (mid-1800s to 1900)
Emphasized handicrafts. Features: particular to individual designer, rustic, repeated designs. Example: Oregon Public Library, Illinois.

Art nouveau (late 1800s to mid-1900s)
Emphasized forms found in nature. Features: curvaceous line, arches, Japanese motifs, plant forms, stained glass. Examples: the work of Louis Comfort Tiffany, Louis Sullivan, and Charles Rennie Mackintosh.

Neo-Gothic (1905 to 1930)
Resurgence of Gothic style. Features: pointed windows, gargoyles, long vertical lines, fanciful details formerly used for medieval cathedrals. Example: Woolworth Building, New York City.

Modernism/International (1920s–)
Functional rather than ornamental. Features: glass, steel, and concrete structures. Example: skyscrapers.

Bauhaus (early 1920s to World War II)
Reduced form to its purest. Feature: flat roofs, open floor plans, boxlike forms, strictly functional details. Color is reduced to white, gray, beige, and black. Example: Bauhaus, Dessau, Germany.

Art deco (mid-1920s to mid-1930s)
Employed the simplified forms of Bauhaus and influences of technology. Features: zigzag lines, graduated shapes, emphasis on line, sleek forms. Examples: Chrysler Building and Empire State Building, New York City.

Organic (mid-20th century–)
Buildings suggest natural form and harmony. Features: lack rigidity and formal linear qualities, curves, sustainable practices. Examples: Frank Lloyd Wright's Guggenheim and Saarinen's Kennedy Airport, New York City; Sydney Opera House, Australia.

Assignment 3
historical personality

Similar to customer profiling and using period fashion for inspiration, this assignment explores people and the "tribe" they are associated with.

△ Sheer artistry
The spirit of Frida Kahlo is captured in this collection through the interpretations of ethnic dress. Using modern fabrics and silhouettes ensure a collection maintains currency for today's customer, no matter which period is researched.

How do color, fabric, silhouette, and detail communicate a personality? How can a historical icon and aspects of period dress inform and modernize fashion design? How can a persona portray the lifestyle marketed by a designer?

The success of a collection based on a historical personality depends on how deep and contextualized the period and icon research is. The context of the period the icon lived in and how they related to it should be considered. The personal achievements that made them iconic and how they may inform a personality for today are also important.

■ AIMS

- Learn how color, fabric, silhouette, and detail communicate a personality
- Understand how a persona can contribute to the aspirational lifestyle marketed by designers today
- Recontextualize a period icon to create a contemporary collection

Using Anastasia Romanov, the daughter of Czar Nicholas II, as the inspiration for a collection, one student discovered that Anastasia was considered the tomboy of the Russian royal family. Focusing on this character trait, an athletic-wear collection was designed.

In order to provide a design concept and visual juxtaposition for the collection, Russian military uniforms from the pre-Revolutionary period of 1915–1917, along with the aristocratic women's fashions of the time that were dominated by Parisian design houses, were synthesized to symbolize the opposing views of the period between the aristocrats and the revolutionaries.

Various weights of jersey fabric, along with nylons and cottons, supported the athletic-wear category; pastel colors and shades of white maintained the feminine and period aesthetic to soften the masculine, military garment details, such as epaulettes, military pockets, and hardware, including exaggerated snap closures and D-rings.

Possible icons to research:

Ghenghis Khan
Joan of Arc
Boudicca
Napoleon
Daisy or Jordan, *The Great Gatsby*
Josephine Bonaparte
Queen Elizabeth I
Annie Oakley
Virginia Woolf
Madame de Pompadour
Edgar Allan Poe
Captain Bligh
Sacajawea
Catherine the Great
Doctor Zhivago
Madame Butterfly
Frida Kahlo
Anastasia Romanov
King Arthur
Lewis and Clark
Jane Austen
Mata Hari

▪ METHOD

When building your design process, try to follow these steps:

1 Select your icon Your selection should be universally known and iconographic, and can be fictional or nonfictional.

2 Step outside of predetermined gender-based collections For example, how could a womenswear collection be derived from Ghenghis Khan? How could a menswear collection be based on Amelia Earhart?

3 Research and create two mood boards
On the left side, show your icon as they were then. Consider composing your research from artwork, period interiors they inhabited, text, and historical garments. On the right, compose images of your character's speculated lifestyle in today's world, using similar types of image contexts.

4 Consider color, print, fabric, proportions, silhouette, and construction
How do they contribute to how we perceive the wearer? How can fabric weights and textures communicate a personality? Is brevity of detail and texture or intricate detail most representative of your icon? Were your icons ahead of their time and likely to appreciate advanced textile technologies, or were they more representative of the norms during their period?

5 Complete the croquis process Focus on the psychology of your icon. What shapes will be favored and why? How referentially must period detail be depicted? Would your character favor more tailored or organic silhouettes? How will you allocate these two percentages within the collection, and why? What lifestyle and personality attributes will inform the collection's usage and context within present-day fashion?

Assignment 4
ethnic background

This assignment explores how a regionalized costume that may denote a hierarchy, religious affiliation, or delineations within a community can be adapted for today's fashion consumer.

▨ AIMS

- Research ethnic dress and notions of community
- Analyze design aspects of national dress
- Adapt traditional designs to today's customer

From the folkloric embroideries of the Ukraine and the neck rings worn by the Kayan people, to the wealth and color of body adornments exhibited by the ancient Mayan culture, a costume often offers an extreme representation of a localized society. Displaying social hierarchies, as seen in the tribes of North America, and sometimes used to eradicate status by communicating a homogenized community, as with the Quakers and present-day Amish, a society's costume is as much about using the resources available as it is about how a community communicates its social frameworks.

EXAMPLES OF ETHNIC DRESS

Regional costume varies not only within the geographic locations of the world, but also within their particular communities. Although shapes, fabrics, and details may differ, consider what kinds of similarities may exist in neighboring communities, as well as those shared by areas of similar climates.

The Americas

Biil	Navajo
Serape	Mexico
Guayabera	Cuba
Pilcha	Brazil
Huaso costume	Chile
Pollera	Panama

Europe

Aboyne dress	Scotland
Lederhosen	Germany
Dirndl	Austria
Subu	Hungary
Riza	Bulgaria
Sarafan	Russia
Bunad	Norway
Sverigedrakten	Sweden
Fustanella	Greece
Entari	Turkey

Africa

Dashiki	West Africa
Caftan	Morocco
Galebeya	Egypt
Kamis	Ethiopia

Asia

Djellaba	Arabia
Kurta	Afghanistan
Shalwar kameez	South Asia
Choga	India
Angarkha	Pakistan
Ao dai	Vietnam
Sampot	Cambodia
Songket	Malaysia
Tapis	Indonesia
Del	Mongolia
Chuba	Tibet
Gho	Bhutan
Hanfu	China
Hanbok	Korea
Kimono	Japan

◁ **Out of Africa** Colors, symbols, and ceremonial adornment provide conceptual meaning for development. Consider how materials used across the world carry different associations.

▷ **Local folk** Indigenous crafts provide extensive material for inspiration. A pattern's color relationships, shapes, scale, and meanings vary greatly from culture to culture.

■ METHOD

Research an ethnic background and use your inspiration to build a collection by keeping the following criteria in mind:

1 Select one focus This will not only keep the group's narration cohesive, but encourage you to research at a fairly deep and contextual level to acquire enough material. However, for another type of assignment, it could be exciting to use two different types of background to see how they juxtapose, as demonstrated in the polarities assignment on pages 118–119.

2 Historical narration Investigate the era and the location from which the national dress arose.

• Was it a period of wealth for the particular society?
• Did the community build relationships with other nations or remain insular?
• Was it a time of war and conflict?
• Did religious beliefs influence dress?
• How could these ideas be incorporated into the collection's design development?

3 Design criteria Examine, through the visual and physical attributes of costume, what makes your community distinct from others in the geographic vicinity. Textiles, garment silhouettes, appropriation and usage of dress, color palette, handicrafts and techniques for costume embellishment, and even cues that are not garment related—such as body painting/adornment—can provide criteria from which to extrapolate design information.

4 Adaptation Referencing the customer profile, consider what type of consumer would prefer a literal translation, and which customers would appreciate an adaptation of a localized costume that retains the designer's signature colors, fabrics, and silhouettes. Analyze your customer's needs to inform how color is to be handled and how the levels of interpretation should be conveyed. For example, the rich primary colors of Eastern European costume could turn into tonal, gray-based pastels for a more subtle and texture-focused collection. Decide if your customer would prefer a traditional, familiar silhouette or one that has been manipulated.

5 Relevancy The final design must be one that is influenced by an inspiration, but takes several steps away from its original location to acquire the "signature" of the particular designer. Make the work your own vision, and not simply a copied reflection of it.

▷ **Straps and stripes** The physical motifs of the Jewish tallit and tefillin provide this collection with a directional motif. Printed stripes provide literal context, and a stripe effect is seen in layered shirts. Wrapped straps are suggested through actual fabric strips and seamed pants. The two are synthesized in the sweater in the top right corner.

Assignment 5
opposite designer

This assignment looks at achieving objectivity by building a collection that is unfamiliar in colors, fabrics, construction methods, details, and silhouettes for a different customer audience.

■ AIMS

- Investigate a designer's creative development
- Analyze the work's artistic hallmarks
- Develop objectivity by designing in another designer's aesthetic

Although often beginning with personal aesthetic and a feeling for what the upcoming collection must possess, designers draw upon their abilities to objectively review their collections before final presentation while always remaining cognizant in solidifying their brand's identity. When viewing another designer's collections, analyze the body of work as a whole and cite areas that are weak or successful. By learning to ask questions with such specificity, you will gain a framework for critique that you can apply to your own work, thereby strengthening your creative practice.

△ ▷ **In close range** Despite the similar palette of grays and pinks, these two collections represent profoundly different aesthetics through the extremities of silhouette and inspiration interpretation that help define the collection's mood and customer.

◁ **Graphic relationships** Keeping color relationships with sharper graphic contrast creates a younger, more casual feeling than a subtle, tonal palette. This collection uses less texture emphasis and relies on complex color relationships for its design focus.

■ METHOD

1 Choose an "opposite" Ask an outsider, perhaps someone who knows your aesthetic and methodologies for working, to assign you an "opposite." Factors that will help an outsider to determine this opposite could include the types of inspiration you frequently use, research cited, colors and fabrics favored, how you address print and texture, silhouettes and construction techniques that frequently provide hallmarks of your sensibilities, and the customer you address.

2 Research the opposite's work Create a board of images from previous collections that best represent their creative vision. It is important to show a well-edited source of images that summarizes an overall "umbrella" of aesthetic direction.

• How practical is the approach to design?
• How are silhouettes frequently handled?
• How is color used and what emotions are associated with the commonly used palettes?
• What is the general mood of the customer being addressed?
• What types and levels of inspiration are synthesized, and how are they manifested in the collection?

3 Apply the inspiration to your customer Determine an inspiration that is in keeping with how the designer formulates a collection and that will address your customer's aesthetic. How conceptual, visual, and literal a designer must be when contextualizing research is largely governed by this particular aesthetic and customer base.

4 Create the collection Objectively create a cohesive collection that remains true to the house's iconic representation and purpose through design, yet one that also pushes the label forward to avoid repeating itself, all the while remaining relevant to the current fashion climate.

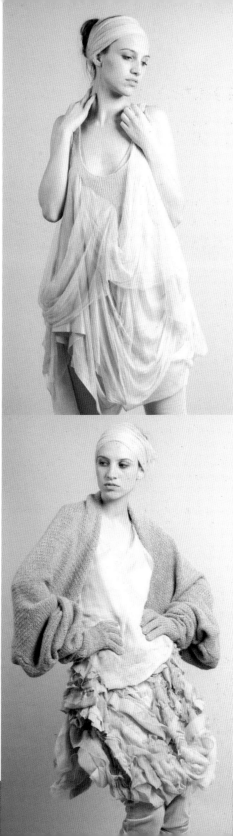

Consider the following criteria when evaluating professional collections:

• Are both construction and fabric in agreement?
• Is this one-stop shopping? Is the collection well merchandised?
• Are the silhouettes and fabrics season appropriate?
• How is texture and pattern handled?
• Are there enough fabric weights?
• How well edited is the group? Is there redundancy (silhouette, fabric, etc.), or room for expansion?
• How do the fabrics and silhouettes adhere to the inspiration? Are they effective in this?
• How well defined is the customer? How could the definition be made firmer?
• How are "editorial pieces" used within the group, if at all?
• What would you have done to make the group stronger?

◁ **Tone on tone** The harmonious tones of this collection's palette underscore the complex textural emphasis. Mohair, cashmere, and cotton in varying knit gauges remain the focus because of minimal color contrast.

Assignment 6

swap

As part of a design team, you'll need to know how to work effectively within the team dynamic. This assignment will encourage you to work methodically and objectively with another designer's inspiration and concept.

■ AIMS

- Synthesize design ideas
- Negotiate contrary views
- Increase your creative range through objective analysis and stepping out of your comfort zone

As members working in a creative team, designers convene frequently to discuss the direction for a collection's focus during all stages of development. A designer should be able to traverse diverse aesthetics and propose his or her point of view within a pre-outlined framework when building a collection.

This assignment imagines the participants as a design director and design-team member. The director researches an inspiration and prescribes it to the design-team member. The mood board and fabrics are well formulated by the director, providing an axis that the design-team member can expand upon, within the parameters of the original criteria.

▷ **Balancing act** The "goth" aesthetic frequently seen in this student's work was challenged when the student was assigned a more colorful and textured palette to design from. The assigned category of juniors is conveyed through whimsical color combinations, rich textural details, and feminine silhouettes.

Design one

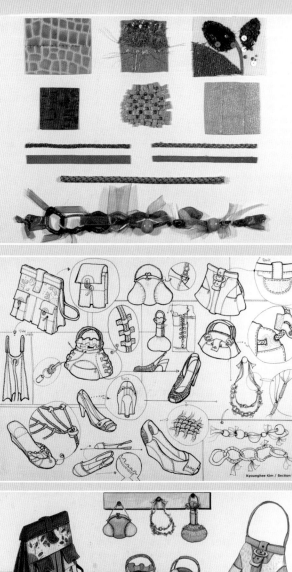

Design two

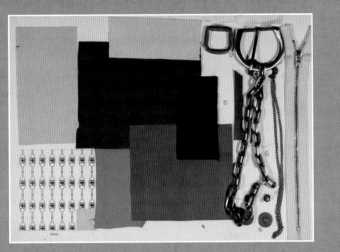

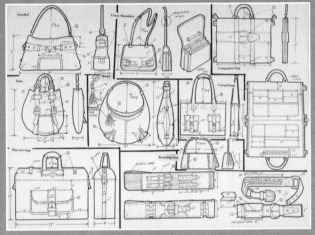

◼ METHOD

Each participant should create a mood board and a fabric board based on the inspiration. There must not be more than twelve swatches per fabric board, including at least two coating weights, two suiting weights, two blouse/shirt weights, one to two novelty fabrics, and various cut-and-sew and sweater weights. The season may be fall/winter or spring/summer.

1 Assign and swap the boards As a group, review the boards and pair up participants who will swap their boards, ensuring an opposite aesthetic, theme, color, and fabric palette is assigned to each designer.

2 Meet up Board creators meet with their recipients to discuss the theme, customer, and other aesthetic aspects the creator intends the collection to convey, so that the recipient has sufficient information and may research additional images to develop context for the design process.

3 Create a collection All fabrics on the board must be used when designing the collection. However, before beginning the design process, two fabrics may be replaced with alternatives to make the fabric palette stronger.

4 Present to the "director" When forty to fifty croquis are completed, edit and illustrate six to eight looks to represent the group. The board creator and designer discuss the evolution of the collection with the group for a critique, and the group will analyze the intended direction in the same way that design directors would offer feedback to their design team.

◁ **Desert trail** Earthy colors and utilitarian construction give this grouping its focused character. Stepping out of a comfort zone teaches you to design objectively so that design can be highly resolved and meet the needs of your audience, no matter what your personal preferences.

Assignment 7
nature

Nature is perhaps the most universal theme designers can appropriate for their collections. Here you will be guided through working with the theme, from initial concept to building a coherent collection.

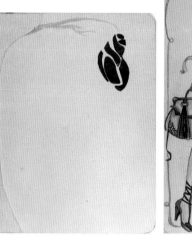

From direct manifestations, such as the development of a color palette that references the colors of the Sahara, to concepts that can be used for garments that mimic an armadillo's segmented structure, nature can inform a collection from the most simple and primary level to the most innovative and conceptual. In its most sophisticated representation, nature often relies on the suggestion of a reference, rather than a literal manifestation.

The inspiration must be investigated at a fairly granular level and then restructured through the designer's own lens, so that the point of origin serves to provide focus. To simply appliqué seashell shapes onto a garment may not be the most advanced method for interpreting research. However, by investigating the shells' internal and external structures, patterns, three- and two-dimensional shapes, and even the lifestyle of the creature that inhabits them, a designer may be influenced when devising a collection and use these visual cues in a highly personalized manner.

▨ AIMS

- Interpret natural elements to inform design decisions
- Grasp how to expand your inspiration to include a nonliteral influence

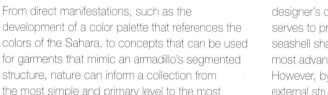

■ METHOD

Build a collection based on themes and concepts of nature by considering the following criteria:

1 Color palette The colors provided may offer a highly resolved color palette that matches both fabric choices and the intended aesthetic of the collection. However, consider building a color palette that is not directly related to your inspiration. In doing so you avoid the pitfalls of using the research and theme too literally.

2 Fabric development Consider how your inspiration can inform fabric design through prints, manipulations, dyeing techniques, beading, color blocking, and other decorative elements.

3 Silhouettes Create levels of design intensity to allow for one-stop shopping: Some looks may involve a more fashion-forward construction, fabric, and wearability, whereas others must provide for a less involved experience, such as a familiar pant or skirt silhouette and tailored shirt with subtle detail that relates to the inspiration.

4 Put them all together Consider how the shape, color, texture, line, and form of your natural inspiration could be manipulated in various forms of motif.

◁ **Balanced** Embroidered thorns give this chiffon sheath dress by Sophia Kokosalaki the right balance of delicacy and subversion. The suggestion of a Rorschach ink blot through the use of positive shape further contextualizes the meaning behind the chosen motif.

▽ **Butterfly house** The intricate form of a butterfly wing serve as the motif for this day-to-night collection. Using a nonreferential color palette helps to avoid the pitfalls of appearing too literal in inspiration interpretation.

Assignment 8
3D/2D

For some designers, a vision of form always precedes the two-dimensional design process. The following assignment will familiarize you with working fluidly between the two- and three-dimensional elements of design.

■ AIMS

- Incorporate three-dimensional design with the two-dimensional process
- Experiment with draping fabric to advance your collection

Silhouette, method of construction, and three-dimensional motifs may be the underlying context for building a collection. Other aspects of the design process could involve experimentation in the appropriate fabric weight. Some drapes may be based on a particular motif you have in mind, whereas others may convey a mood or "experience" that the garment will give the wearer.

■ METHOD

Once an inspiration has been researched and conceptualized:

1 Drape and pin Choose an appropriate fabric weight, such as medium-weight muslin, to pin onto the dress form. As you work through various forms and fabric manipulations, document each progression from various angles and proximities with a camera or by other means. Depending on the drape, a particular portion may lend itself to other aspects of the garment.

2 Consider the following points when working on the dress form:

- How can the types of drape vary from the strictly 2D, such as seaming detail, to the more sculptural 3D, such as full skirts or draped effects? How can the middle ground also be explored, such as pleated or origami effects?
- When changing fabric weights, try draping the same form executed in the earlier fabric weight to investigate how it may create cohesion for the collection.
- Work with various proportions of the same drape on the form to determine which is most successful.

3 Documentation Document the process with each significant transition from various angles and proximities to the form. A fully documented 360-degree view of the figure may be required, depending on what elements you wish to investigate later on.

4 Build the collection When six to eight drapes have been well documented, select three or four that will provide reference when designing the collection. Although this research will present one level of context, it is important to use your inspiration as the primary focus and to synthesize the two criteria together so that your collection's theme is successfully conveyed. Do not mount the documented images until your design process is finished, as you will need to reference them easily while you design. Be sure to use both the more 2D drapes and the sculptural 3D drapes so you challenge your ability to incorporate two effects successfully in the collection.

◁ **Forms for discussion** Documenting both sculptural and linear styles of drape gives designers a diverse and balanced selection to work from. Like motif, drapes must be used in varying scales, fabrics, and placements on the body.

PROFESSIONAL EXAMPLE

The three-dimensional process is essential when a design can be appreciated only in its full rotation, as seen in the geometric work of Geoffrey Beene. Before becoming a highly focused fashion designer, Beene was a medical student, and his reference to the body was three-dimensional, rather than the blank page where a front and back design would be drawn. Given this context, his work frequently incorporates seaming, negative space, and other geometric motifs that wrap around the body and can be fully appreciated only when the design is in full 360-degree rotation.

◁ △ **Momentary fragments** Textile development swatches can be tested for scale and placement during the design process. This knitted swatch is manipulated through varying scales and shapes on diverse silhouettes for merchandising purposes.

△ **Gestural beginnings** Designers occasionally begin with silhouette gestures before delving into the design process. Gestures provide a structure for the collection's direction and convey the overarching message for the particular season.

Assignment 9
macro to micro

A common trait among designers is their ability to notice the smallest detail and how it contributes to the whole. This assignment explores the relationship of the specific and the general, and how they support one another through design, color, texture, mood, and usage.

■ AIMS
- Exercise your attention to detail
- Encourage you to question design relationships more thoroughly

▽ **Erecting the scaffolding**
A bold linear quality unifies this collection. Maintaining familiar silhouettes emphasizes complex design relationships.

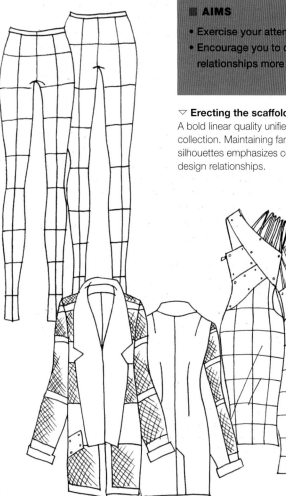

From observing texture and color on the city streets and accumulating the visual information for use in a collection, to seeing a period garment detail that can be modernized and appropriated in their own work, when developing a collection, a designer must always be able to collect the most granular of detail and relate it to the grander scale.

The size of a button, the sound a fabric makes, how a garment is put on, the finishing for a hem, and even the type of cording used for a drawstring must all be selected with great care to fully resolve a garment and contribute to the collection's aesthetic.

◁ **Construction ahead** The forms, textures, colors, and shapes of a construction site provided inspiration for this denim collection. The balance of color and varied silhouettes, along with a customer-appropriate color palette, give dynamic results.

■ METHOD

1 Document an environment Use a camera to record the general macro of an environment, such as your bedroom, a building's lobby, an office, a restaurant, or an alleyway. These images will be used for color and overall mood when developing the customer profile. Historical sites, buildings that represent an iconic art or design movement, and other spaces that have a clearly unified aesthetic are best. Then document selected "micro," or details, of the space that inspire you. These will be used for design areas such as motif, fabric treatments, details, silhouette, print development, and knitwear stitches. Three to four details is a good number for the final edits to use in the collection.

2 Macro Base your color palette on the room or environment and the customer: Who is the woman/man who inhabits this space? For some designers this could mean a literal representation, whereas others may rely more heavily on the environment's mood. For example, a particular restaurant may provide specificity of customer given its type of menu, location, and ambience. Other spaces, such as an alleyway, could provide a unique mood given the neighborhood it is in, colors and textures found, abundance (or lack of) natural light, and other visual clues that can be used to create an imaginary customer.

3 Micro Use the micro details in various scales, fabrics, 3D and 2D applications, and color relationships, such as tonal and graphic. Vary the level of interpretation from the directly referenced to the suggestion of the shapes, textures, or forms documented. Using these guidelines will add design depth to the collection while maintaining cohesion through motif. Similar to accent colors, the micro details used must not all play equally in design attention. Let one dominate and the other(s) recede to prevent an overly designed collection that appears unfocused.

4 Build the collection When composing your six to eight edits from the croquis, analyze the order of the looks from left to right in terms of narration, color flow, accent color proportion and placement on the body, merchandising, variety of design intensity, tailored with organic silhouette, and one-stop shopping. It is also essential to offer levels of inspiration interpretation.

Assignment 10
concept to runway

The following assignment explores the levels of inspiration interpretation, how a collection is developed, and how it is adapted for practicality.

■ AIMS

- Use extreme or literal representations of your inspiration to set the tone, attitude, and aspiration of your product
- Filter a concept down from its most representational form to a more mass-marketable product
- Determine successful orders of runway presentation

When building a collection, it is essential to consider the order in which the looks are presented. How momentum is built, how a color and silhouette is manipulated, and the various devices employed to convey concept and inspiration give the collection focus and cohesion. How designers narrate the interpretation of a theme may vary, however. For some, the sequence of a presentation may tell a story from look to look, each building one upon another; conventional silhouettes may begin the story that soon morphs into extreme examples of the concept, a technique frequently employed by Alexander McQueen. Other designers may create a presentation order that has various peaks spread throughout the show, where a saturated representation of concept or inspiration is filtered among the other levels of interpretation.

CONSIDER THE FOLLOWING FORMULA WHEN COMPOSING A COLLECTION:

20 percent pure or "extreme" representation

Representing the purity of a concept, inspiration, and vision for the collection, this group contains items that are either for editorial and runway use only, or are the more literal manifestations of the designer's themes. For some designers these may be highly artistic creations that are unlikely to be mass-produced, such as the robotic pieces of Hussein Chalayan, or wearable garments that are highly evocative of an inspiration, such as the ornate ethnic embroideries executed at Oscar de la Renta.

60 percent core body

The largest of the three areas within a collection, the "core body" defines the designer's identity for consumers, consisting of the primary pieces retailers will buy for their stores. The design intensity range within this category must also vary from the literal to the more filtered representations of the theme, but the items must remain saleable and design driven.

20 percent basics

No matter how forward thinking and avant-garde the designer may be, "basics" are always offered within the collection. From iconic T-shirts and the familiar suit, to core silhouettes that may include basic pants and skirts with minimal detail, this area gives your less fashion-forward customers an opportunity to be a part of your aspirational world while also providing your loyal customers with a full wardrobe for one-stop shopping.

△ **It's a wrap** Inspired by a building's steel structure, these highly conceptualized looks include tattooed lines that turn into wire and wrap around the wearer and knitted wool with silver filament that protects the figure against the elements.

◁ **Adapting a concept** Using a specific motif in varying fabrics, weights, and scales prevents redundancy and monotony of design. Varying color relationships also contribute to creating a well-formulated collection that addresses the need for one-stop shopping.

■ METHOD

1 Start pure Begin the croquis process with literal (pure) representations of your inspiration and concept. Bear in mind that these initial sketches do not necessarily need to relate to one another through motif, fabric, and color, because design elements will be extrapolated for the two other "filtered" categories that make up the majority of the collection. You might consider these looks for actual production, or they could simply be one-of-a-kinds that add to the show dramatically and contextually.

2 Adapt for core body As you design the second, core section, consider how the most extreme looks may be modified in silhouette, detail, fabric, or other criteria to make them accessible to a broader audience. Adapt the intensities of design as you progress and merchandise. Design may be simplified, proportions modified, color relationships altered and made less intense, fabrics substituted for wearability, and fabric treatments adjusted in proportion or method of execution. Consider how styling can play an important role in conveying a varied intensity of inspiration and concept.

3 Develop the basics From the previous two categories, the third and final grouping is developed. This category is made up of items that are universal to all designers and markets, yet fit within your collection by means of color, fabric, and a more generalized aesthetic. Examples include the iconic man's-style shirt, T-shirts, basic pants and skirts, and other pieces that may seem generic on their own, yet remain cohesive in your collection's context. They serve as foundation pieces in your group and can be seamlessly added to a customer's existing wardrobe.

4 Runway order Beginning with a rough layout of twelve to fifteen figures, start to determine the presentation order. Consider building up to a crescendo at the end, when the most literal and extreme silhouettes are displayed, or devise a show where highs and lows are filtered throughout to add occasional drama. Once the order is determined, decide where core basics will be needed to support the other two categories, and allow for the diverse experiences that the customer will want when wearing your collection.

Assignment 11
shifts in fashion

Through the examination of the societal forces that brought about evolutions and revolutions in fashion design, this assignment explores the physical manifestation of conceptual ideals that were often contrary to their prevailing societal norms.

▉ AIMS

- Analyze how a shift in design can influence a culture's future and provide the impetus for lifestyle changes
- Use a shift from fashion history to inform your own collection

How women were viewed and their position in society, how the changing political and economical global structures enabled change, and the advent of new technologies are just a few examples of external forces that propelled fashion forward and gave new meanings to what one wore. Such "shifts" gave rise to the diversity of fashion "tribes," and how one dressed moved from simply indicating social class to exhibiting one's personality, beliefs, and group affiliations.

POSSIBLE CONCEPTS TO RESEARCH:

- The denim and daywear of Claire McCardell
- The emphasis of architectural shape and form devoid of superfluous detail (Balenciaga, Zoran, Sybilla, Montana, etc.)
- The global economy and its influence on ethnic-inspired fashion
- "The Japanese invasion" during the 1980s in Paris
- French new wave or beatnik culture
- Futurism (Cardin, Courrèges, etc.)
- Hippie and/or British punk ideology
- Menswear as womenswear (1920s fashion, *Annie Hall*, early Armani, etc.)
- The influence of the military in ready-to-wear (World War I, World War II, Vietnam, historical, etc.)
- Technological advancements in fabric development and manufacturing
- The use of nontraditional/unconventional materials and/or utilitarianism (Paco Rabanne, Martin Margiela, Thierry Mugler, Prada's nylon, Kamali's parachute silk, etc.)

▽ **Sepia tones** A montage of historical sepia prints of corseted figures influenced the color palette.

▷ **Positive influence**
Gabrielle "Coco" Chanel rejected the corset, which required a woman to be dependent on someone else to dress her and restricted her movement. Chanel's use of jersey fabric advocated a more active lifestyle that was less constrained in both physical and societal terms.

◁ **Softening up** Irony gives this collection a dose of humor as well as a clear commentary. The rigidity of the corset is rethought through soft shapes and fabrics in this cozy knitwear group.

APPLY THE RESEARCH TO DESIGN

Consider the following when working through the design process:

• What "norms" were prevalent before the shift, and how can these be incorporated into the collection to provide context and juxtaposition?

• How do color and fabric visually represent the historical shift?

• How does the inspiration relate to the shift? Does it need to?

• How reliant is silhouette development on the shift, and would the customer respond to literal or abbreviated interpretations?

• Was the current female ideal redefined as part of this shift? Does this inform your customer?

• What norms of dress occurred during the shift? How can these silhouettes be used as the foundation for the shift?

• What movement occurred after the shift? Were there any attributes that carried over to the following era's shift that influenced society?

■ METHOD

Research a shift in fashion history that you respond to for its design principle and aesthetic:

1 Societal influences Research how society provided the impetus for such a revolution and what the elements were that the shift rebelled against.

2 Expand on inspiration Although the shift selected is meant to provide a general concept and influence for your collection, you must then develop and research an inspiration of your own. For example, menswear as womenswear could be your concept with art-deco furniture as your design inspiration.

ASSIGNMENT 12
polarities

This assignment explores the relationship between extreme opposites of a joint theme.

AIMS

- Expose you to researching two concepts related to one theme
- Teach you how to discover and develop inspiration from a concept
- Allow you to create a much larger context of theme in a collection
- Encourage you to think about the inspiration balance in clothing

For some designers, combining two opposite moods, feelings, or ideas can result in the creation of a third that bridges seemingly opposite aesthetics. This creates a collection that is diverse in silhouette, color, texture, and pattern, yet remains cohesive in its main themes. Where your collection begins and where it ends may be very different, but the order of the runway exits in between give a thematic connection. It is also essential to learn how intense or subtle a reference can be used. Some of your looks may be very focused toward one of the themes, whereas other looks may be very focused toward the other. Those that are mixed may have a ratio of influence: 75/25, 50/50, 25/75.

▷ The designer was inspired by the polarities "Order/Disorder."

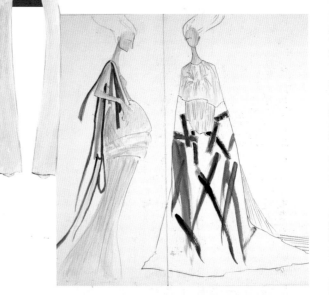

Sample Polarities:

- Organic/Linear
- Classic/Avant-garde
- Utilitarian/Luxury
- Reveal/Conceal
- Local/Foreign
- Macro/Micro
- Internal/External
- Constructed/Deconstructed
- Masculine/Feminine
- Conformist/Rebel
- Fluid/Hard

METHOD

1 Choose polarities Select a pair of concepts from the panel, left; for example, "Organic/Linear."

2 Select a theme Now that you have selected your concepts, you must gather your inspiration. For "Organic/Linear," an appropriate inspiration theme could be art: art nouveau for Organic, and art deco for Linear. These two design movements have defined shapes, color palettes, textures, and forms associated with them, and will give you a large quantity of research material. They are also both used in furniture, decorative arts, even graphic design—allowing for more direct comparisons.

As you research the movements, notice how their design applications differ in color, form, scale, and texture. How are they similar? How would your fabric choices remain distinct from each other, and where would there be an overlap of shared fabrics or colors?

3 Create your palettes From there, create a fabric palette that represents both "opposites" and decide where colors or fabrics will bridge the two polarities.

STUDENT EXAMPLE

Concept: Order/disorder
Inspiration: Artists Barnett Newman (order) and Franz Kline (disorder). In this example, "Order/Disorder" was selected as the polarity, with "art" and "movement" as sample themes to research. The artist Barnett Newman was known for his large color-field paintings that gave a feeling of control, line, uniformity, and military precision. There is a lack of movement in his brushwork, and his compositions are very "ordered." Franz Kline, on the other hand, applied paint in an almost violent, kinetic manner with complete disregard for controlled shape or boundaries. His work is not premeditated, and is purely spontaneous in the paint's application and form. This schism is also captured in the difference between a militaristic march and fluid ballet.

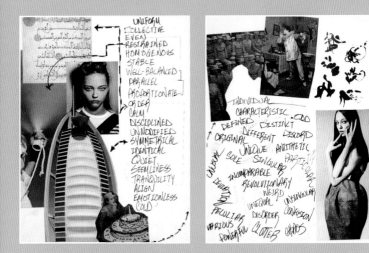

◁ **Word associations**
Listing words for how the collection should feel can keep you focused when making fabric, color, and design decisions. This student created a list describing the two opposite polarities and accentuated their meaning through placement on the page alongside well-edited images.

◁ **Using movement for inspiration** The student defined the concept through types of movement: a military march for the "order" (providing the student with military details), and the emotional ballet of Nijinsky for the "disorder" (providing the student with the ballet tutu as a silhouette).

▷ **Sketch development: Newman-inspired order**
When we look at the sketch development of the group, the "Newman" portion is linear in garment shape and militaristic in detail. Long collars, plackets, coats, and even figure pose lend themselves to a more controlled, linear, and vertical feeling.

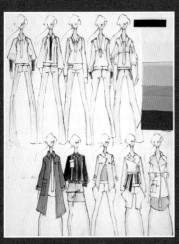

◁ **Sketch development: Kline-inspired disorder**
The "Kline" portion breaks up the figure with horizontals to move our eye, fabric silhouettes and treatments that move, and construction that segments the body. These all result in a chaotic composition and a looser silhouette.

Assignment 13

one inspiration for an entire class

Learning through others' work is essential when developing as a designer. This group assignment takes a single inspiration as an axis that each designer uses to create his or her own collection.

The inspiration prescribed for building a collection should never deter designers from embracing the subject matter in order to create a collection that displays their own unique and creative thumbprint. Fabrics, colors, and the inspiration itself can all be handled in a way that allows designers to best express themselves, rather than the criteria imposing its personality on the designer.

AIMS

- Discover new methods for forming collections by observing other designers' processes
- Learn how an inspiration is interpreted
- Learn how research is performed and edited
- Become aware of the criteria for merchandising a collection

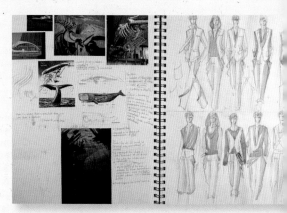

◁ △ **Sailing the seven seas** Avoiding period dress as reference, this *Moby-Dick*-inspired collection uses the whaling ship's rigging and sail shapes to create a refined menswear group through innovative construction and detail.

■ METHOD

1 Assign a broad thematic "umbrella" for the theme and inspiration, and then allow the participants to extrapolate various elements that they will research further to build a context of their own.

2 When the projects have been completed and are presented, consider the following in each collection and compare these with the other approaches shown:

- How was a framework of research built? How did the conceptual development lead to the specific areas of research pursued?
- What decisions were made for fabric and color choices, and how were they made?
- How close in interpretation is the collection to the theme? Does this relate effectively to the customer addressed? Why or why not?
- What types of conceptual idea were used when developing the group? How do they speak to the theme? How were the concepts related to design?
- How diverse were the types of customer among the projects? Does one type lend itself more to the theme than another type? Why or why not?
- How can the most dissimilar approaches from your own personal interpretation of the theme enhance your future design process?
- Are there projects that look similar in their final execution but used seemingly diverse "pathways?" Did any of the projects begin with additional research that was similar but then become radically different in their final outcomes?
- How did the illustration and methods of presentation contribute to customer definition?
- What types of market were represented and how were these categories supported through fabric choice? How do construction methods enhance the category?
- Did the inspiration influence the price point of the collection? Why? How?
- Compare the projects that were more closely related to the inspiration and those that were several "levels" away from direct reference. How does this affect the customer addressed?

▷ **Ahab's crew** The artwork of Rockwell Kent gives this collection its design direction while using *Moby-Dick* for inspiration. Through period menswear, a relaxed attitude, and updated proportions, a casual downtown customer is conveyed.

Assignment 14

accessories

As one of the largest emerging markets in fashion design, accessories complement a designer's collection and offer core customers one-stop shopping. This assignment takes you through all you need to know to create your own successful accessories.

■ AIMS

- Familiarize yourself with existing accessory collections
- Explore the various approaches toward accessory design
- Consider which approach is best applied to your collection and why

Although clothing is always at the forefront, accessories are carefully considered and are an integral part of the retail and sales experience. How each design house approaches the process for accessory design can be profoundly diverse. For some, the accessories grouping stands on its own and remains seemingly unrelated to the motifs and themes of the clothing designed, whereas others are conceived and designed directly from the colors, motifs, and fabrics of the clothes, to support the overall presentation for the consumer and retail experience.

▽ **Texture play** Fabrics often serve to complement a look through unexpected textures such as these pony-hair shoes and eel-skin clutch.

■ METHOD

For each approach listed here, research the example work given and then find your own examples.

1 Primary focus Designers and labels who began their corporations as suppliers of leather goods and fashion accessories have increasingly begun to produce small capsules of clothing to expand their offerings to their core customers while also attracting new ones. The accessories are generally designed first, with clothing added later so the customer identity may be further solidified in a secondary manner.
Examples: Coach, Cole Haan, Bally, Kate Spade

2 Secondary focus To maintain focus on the house's signature clothing design, accessories are designed directly from the collection through the extrapolation of motif, color, fabric, and concepts. The same visual elements and thematic direction are appropriated onto accessories, rather than through the creation of separate thematic criteria. The accessories may also be simplified in design and detail to support the collection's mood and customer identity.
Examples: Jil Sander, Calvin Klein, Ralph Lauren

3 Equal emphasis Often gaining initial recognition within the international fashion community as former producers in the small-leather-goods trade, these companies rose to cult status through their seasonal fashion shows that were just as influential as their much-sought-after accessories. Although the house's accessories support the collection's identity, they are often designed as their own unique "package" and represent a tremendous factor in the company's annual revenue.
Examples: Louis Vuitton, Prada, Gucci

4 Solitary focus For those designers who do not expand their corporations with clothing and wish to focus exclusively on accessories, the design process is very similar to that of designing fashion. Small capsule collections that consist of a color and fabric palette may share similar types of hardware and trim detail, and are merchandised based on the variety of product usage, shapes, and times of day.
Examples: Jimmy Choo, Manolo Blahnik, Sigerson Morrison, Christian Louboutin

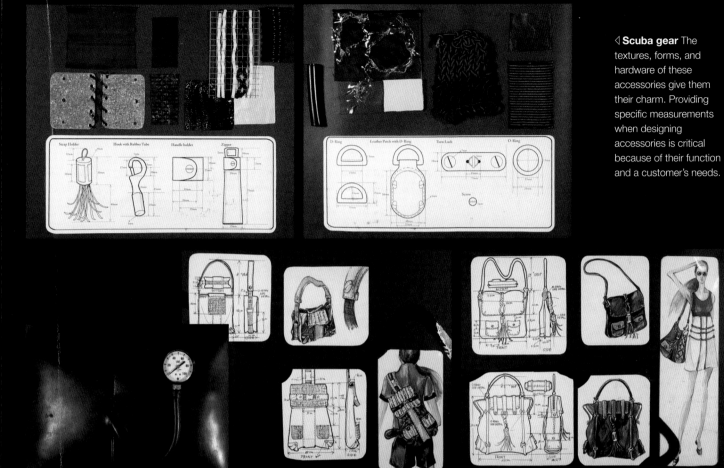

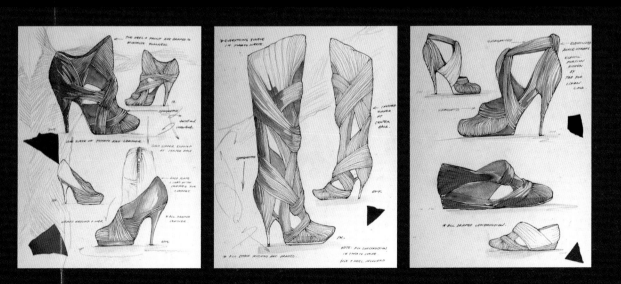

the professional world

The transition between a course in fashion design and the professional world can be a fluid one, provided you have acquired a solid foundation of language, skill, and conceptual thinking as applied to fashion design. Working in the industry during your studies as a design-room intern will provide you with an understanding of how a company operates before you begin as a professional; interning should be thought of as a necessary supplement to your in-class work.

As you move through your academic studies and future career paths, you will become aware of how large the fashion industry is and the types of opportunities it offers. From such direct applications as patternmaking and draping, to areas that use design fundamentals, such as textile design or costume design, and those that use the contextual and academic areas of study, such as fashion journalism and historical studies, the realm of possible careers can suit a wide range of interests and skills.

◁▷ **Making your mark** Students' final-year collections mark their entrance into the professional world. The collection displays all of the skills and concepts mastered, and the area of design that will be pursued.

UNIT 21
career possibilities

The practical and conceptual knowledge that is mastered through the study of fashion design can be applied to a wide range of professional pathways.

It is beneficial during your formative years to discover which areas of fashion and design excite you most and feel most natural. By being sensitive to these signals, you are best placed to find the niche within the industry that most suits your interests and skills.

CONCEPTUAL AND SKILL-BASED ROLES

- **Fashion designer**
Limitless in types of product offered and sizes of design houses. Increasingly global opportunities as major cities around the world host fashion weeks.

- **Textile designer**
Often works within a design house to produce the designs for a collection, or can work for a textile print house that sells exclusive rights to a designer for their seasonal collection.

- **Accessories designer**
Creates products that complement the collection, or may focus on accessories. Suited to those who enjoy the technical and sculptural aspects of design, as well as those who are highly inventive with the engineering aspects.

- **Costume designer**
Strong historical knowledge needed. Adept at using form, fabric, color, and texture to depict a character and mood, particularly in relation to the other personalities within a particular piece of theater or film.

- **Patternmaker/draper/"sample-hand"**
Executes the designer's work, bringing a vision to life. The responsibilities are tremendous and range from simply executing a garment, through assisting in the design to ensure the best solutions for construction, to producing the best technical fit, which can determine retail success or failure.

- **Production manager**
Oversees all samples made for the collection; manages the retailer's orders. From ordering fabric yardage, to tracking the delivery of trims for a garment, and visiting factories and reviewing quality control, managers ensure the product makes it to the stores on time and is of the quality the consumer expects.

- **CAD designer**
Working on fabric prints, supporting the production team on digital garment "specing"—where measurements are supplied to factories for manufacturing—and designing printed graphics for public relations purposes.

- **Stylist**
Aids the designer in accentuating their message. Co-develops fabric and color palettes, assembles runway shows.

ROLES FOCUSING ON KNOWLEDGE AND TRENDS

- **Store buyer**
Knowledge of trends, the store's customer, and how the retail climate fluctuates is critical. Store buyers often have a sixth sense that allows them to know what customers will want months ahead of time.

- **Retail manager**
Knowledge required of fashion at both the current cultural level and the technical level, to inform customers best on the product.

- **Designer showroom representatives**
Work exclusively for the designer and represent the house to store buyers. Knowledge required of the house and product, to meet demands of retailers. Provide feedback to designers for the next season by analyzing sales figures and retailers' requests.

- **Fashion public relations**
Research opportunities for exposure in the media while also ensuring the reputation of the house is maintained through events such as the seasonal collection presentations.

- **Fashion journalist**
Comprehension of fashion history and current events, ability to analyze and critique design, understanding of where fashion is headed.

- **Costume historian**
Undertakes museum or gallery curatorial and research work and garment conservation. Provides students with a deep understanding for fashion design and its societal contexts.

- **Trend forecaster**
Examines the world's current cultural, economic, and sociologic status to predict what changes will occur in the future and how they will affect consumer behavior.

CLOSELY RELATED ROLES

- **Fashion illustrator**
- **Interior designer**
- **Fine artist**
- **Graphic designer**

UNIT 22
the effective résumé

A résumé represents you to prospective employers, often before an in-person meeting occurs. It is essential to impress.

Word choice, organization, visual appeal, neatness, and clarity must all convey to the recipient that you are capable of doing the job, and at a very high level.

A good résumé should serve as a well-stated summary of your experience and skills as they relate to the job you are applying for. Your employment history should show a focused career pathway while highlighting unique experiences that set you apart from the other applicants. The résumé should show your ability to handle responsibility and challenge, and prove that you are an employee who doesn't job-hop every year—employers seek candidates who are interested in building a future with their brand.

It is important to keep in mind that a company often receives scores of applicants. Résumés are scanned over in a matter of seconds, so the ability to stand out through a page design that highlights key areas is pivotal for advancing to the next stage. Given the importance of what this single piece of paper can do for one's professional future, the creation of a successful résumé must be given significant attention.

Résumé Guidelines

Although résumés come in a variety of styles, there are some areas that must be strictly followed for positive representation.

The one-page rule

Unless you have had a previous career, or are in academia, where a multipage curriculum vitae is the norm, keep your résumé to one page in length. It is quick to read by a prospective employer and encourages you to be bold and efficient in word choice and descriptions.

Stand out

Consider how you can "brand" your own identity through the design of your résumé. Given the visual nature of the fashion profession, many prospective employers will respond positively to a well-designed layout. At the same time, use no more than two fonts and avoid excessive graphics— overdesign can hinder clarity.

Be direct

Résumés are often scanned by viewers, but a successful layout will move the eye to the key points, look neat and uniform, and keep information succinct for easy reading.

A light hand

A résumé that is dense with black type appears daunting to read. By allowing for sufficient white spaces the page appears "lighter" to the eye in appearance and has a greater chance of being read. Don't make the viewer work hard to read your résumé.

Time line

The structure of your résumé should read with your most recent employment at the top, and gradually backtrack to the bottom of the page. Line up all of your dates so it is easy for the reader to scan your various histories.

Headings

Commonly used headings are listed in this order: Objective, Education, Experience, Awards, and Skills. Listing volunteer work can also be provided because it shows personal interests and character.

Tense

Use the past tense in all previous places of employment and present in the current. Keep the format in each listing consistent so it looks neat, is easy to read, and allows information to be remembered.

What to omit

Do not list pre-college awards or other criteria. Omit "Résumé" on the page heading, date of birth, and hobbies.

Proofread

Misspelled words, grammatical errors, poor punctuation, and other "slips of the keyboard" will land your résumé in the waste bin. Carelessness is not a desirable trait in new employees, no matter how talented they may be.

UNIT 23
interview
tips and techniques

With sufficient preparation and a few points to remember, an interview is your chance to flaunt your assets more colorfully than a résumé can.

Interviews give you the opportunity to show your personality by demonstrating you are a team player, can contribute significantly to the company, and are a great "fit" with the existing team. Through the presentation of your portfolio and croquis book, elaborating upon professional experiences, and showing your enthusiastic attitude, you can prove you are the one for the job.

Secrets of Success

Here are some pointers for making a great impression in any interview situation, and advice on how to carry that through to the end of the meeting and beyond.

Follow the six rules of interviewing
1 Appear enthusiastic about joining the company.
2 Keep up-to-date on the industry and its competitors in the media.
3 Focus on job responsibilities rather than titles.
4 Research the company thoroughly before entering the interview.
5 Convey your interest in being challenged on the job.
6 Prove you are the consummate team player and one who embraces change.

Do your homework
Your interviewer will ask you for your opinion of their product, what you respond to most about it, and what you think can be improved. Therefore, a visit to their store is a must. Take notes on the merchandise, the store layout, customers, and other elements that you can discuss. Some quick Internet research will give you access to the company's history and any recent press they've received.

Dress the part
Whether you are being interviewed at Gap or Ralph Lauren you should look like a member of their "team." Wearing a look that relates to their aesthetic will communicate your interest in joining their design room and single you out as someone who understands their design process and appears to be a seamless fit.

Arrive ten minutes early
This will allow you to get a feel for the environment, demonstrate that you are punctual, and prevent your interviewer from feeling pressured to see you sooner than planned.

Confidently greet the interviewer
Walk toward your interviewer when they greet you and shake hands firmly while making eye contact. First impressions are made within the first few minutes of meeting so make sure you come across as friendly, professional, and fully engaged.

Mind your body language
Keep both feet flat on the floor and uncrossed, relax your shoulders, face your interviewer, smile, and speak clearly and at an appropriate pace and volume.

The most commonly asked questions
Have an answer ready for these common questions:
• What interests you about the position?
• Why are you looking to leave your employer?
• Tell me about a situation that was challenging for you at work and what you did to resolve it.
• How familiar are you with our company?
• Which designers do you look at and why?
• Where do you see yourself in five years?
• What is your work style?
• What is your greatest weakness/strength?
• If I asked your colleagues to describe you, what would they say?

The three-minute rule
When answering questions, do not talk for more than three minutes, to avoid overexplaining and monopolizing the conversation. Always let your interviewer lead the discussion.

Presenting your work
As you show your portfolio, discuss the elements that make up the particular groups such as color, fabric, and motif, along with the process. Tell the interviewer about how you work, things that appeal to you most about the types of inspiration used, and elements that may not be in your portfolio but contribute to who you are as a designer. Your portfolio must be user-friendly, so avoid loose pages and fold-outs.

Come prepared with questions
By asking thoughtful questions you show you've done your research on the company, are considering the position seriously, and are a proactive employee.

The closing
Thank the interviewer for his or her time and express a specific reason why the position interests you. Shake hands, and thank the receptionist for his or her time as well.

The thank-you note
That same day, send a thank-you note to your interviewer and to all others involved in the interview process. An e-mail might suffice, but there is nothing like receiving a handwritten card through the mail from a candidate.

UNIT 24
portfolio presentation

The portfolio demonstrates the creator's design aesthetic and broad array of abilities.

How collections are conceived, the ability to develop and handle diverse inspiration directions, how colors and fabrics are formulated, attention to detail, computer skill, textile and surface design knowledge, and general organizational abilities are all communicated through this single book. Portfolios must communicate one's versatility of fashion design, yet must also contain groups that are unified in a singular customer identity.

Carefully consider how your portfolio relates to the designer you are interviewing with. Although it should connect strongly to their customer and design aesthetic, it must also appear as an advancement on what they currently do. Designers are often hired for the "fresh eye" they may bring to the current design team, and being a few steps ahead will show you can contribute creatively to the brand.

Sample Sportswear Portfolio

A well-laid-out portfolio should move between groups in a fluid manner. A variety of seasons, categories, and methods of art direction must stimulate the viewer with each consecutive group. For a well-rounded portfolio that is aimed at the sportswear market, consider the following order:

Group 1: Fall/winter tailored sportswear/careerwear

Beginning with a tailored sportswear group provides the viewer with an introduction and a gradual "ease" into your aesthetic. Color palettes are simple in relationships, silhouettes are familiar in shape and predominantly vertical in form, and the collection is not too extreme in inspiration interpretation.

Group 2: Fall/winter sportswear

Includes more complex color and textural relationships, as well as silhouettes that are more unique and diverse. The collection can include a mix of tailored shapes alongside softer silhouettes, and it is often item driven, with pieces that are more "designed."

Group 3: Fall/winter denim, athletic, or knit capsule

The final group allows you to show your range of design versatility and/or a specialty you may have. It must still adhere to the customer you are addressing, however, along with fabrics that speak to the category chosen. It is an opportunity to flaunt a skill you may not have had the opportunity to address yet, such as working with a different color and fabric palette, the design of fashion graphics, technical knowledge associated with knitwear, and various others.

The breather

As a group that divides the seasons, this capsule collection may include an accessory group that speaks to a particular season, remains seasonless, and/or provides the accessories for one of the previous groups. Another option is to provide a resort/holiday group that separates the two seasons and is delivered to stores before the spring and summer collections arrive.

Group 4: Spring/summer tailored sportswear/careerwear

Similar to the first group, the fourth layout addresses tailored sportswear as a transition into spring/summer with a group that is less involved in design relationships. Fabrics allow wearers to stay cool, and color relationships are season-appropriate.

Group 5: Spring/summer sportswear

Consisting primarily of cottons and other fabrics that breathe, and colors that evoke the warmer climate, this group addresses a collection that is more complex in color relationships and/or silhouette. Pieces may transition from career to weekend-wear, and the group is broadly merchandised to offer looks that suit most occasions.

Group 6: Spring/summer evening or high-concept

The final capsule in the portfolio provides the "wow" factor of eveningwear and/or flaunts your creative ability. Color relationships, fabrics, season specificity, and other considerations are largely up to the designer. However, the group adheres to the customer addressed previously, to provide portfolio cohesion and strong aesthetic identity.

◁ **Cover art** Portfolio covers don't need to be generic. Providing an introduction to your aesthetic and creativity supports the internal design work while also exciting your viewer.

▽ **Opting for graphic** The use of a background graphic creates dynamic negative space to move the viewer's eye. A successful layout's art direction supports a design concept without competing with or obstructing the fashion designs.

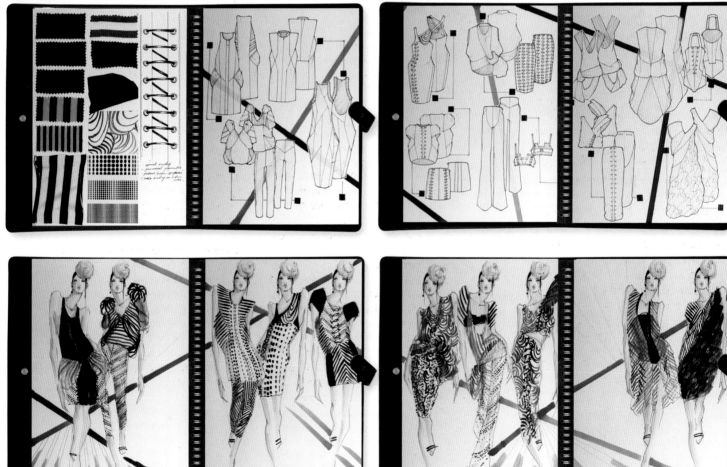

◁ **"The Oval Portrait"** The literary works of Edgar Allan Poe and military uniforms provide mood and ambience in this collection's layout. Photographed nineteenth-century frames and dark forest scenes contrast with the flat, graphic illustrations.

▷ **Aqua Alto** The romance of a trip to Venice is creatively suggested through the use of background and props. Gestural sketches that provide a specified location underscore the richness of the more finished design work.

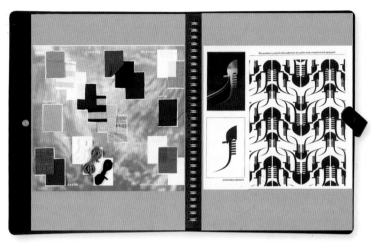

interview: student life

Nathalie Doucet
President of The Arts of Fashion Foundation

As a former designer and educator, Nathalie Doucet has strong insights into how education and the fashion industry can best coalesce. Her foundation promotes the globalization of fashion design by bringing students together so they may study together, display their creative talents to professionals during annual shows and competitions, and attend lectures that discuss the future of fashion design, education practices, and her own personal passion in promoting copyright laws for fashion designers.

△ ▷ **Design methods**
Reexamining existing silhouette through fabric manipulation develops critical skills. This project explores the ways in which motif can be developed.

What does your foundation do, and how does it contribute to students' development as designers?

I created the Arts of Fashion Foundation (AoF) because I discovered while teaching fashion that students have little opportunity for exposure to creative people and the process of creativity in general. The only way for students to be successful is to experience working with creative minds.

Our competitions foster an exchange between over fifty selected high-caliber students, young professionals, and educators from well-respected companies and institutions from all over the world. The CarteBlanche Series comprises three to four rising international designers who are invited to show their work on the runway and also teach five-day master classes. Lectures, seminars, and conversations from educators and professionals are scheduled during the symposium. Topics covering business and education challenges, including copyright and intellectual property in fashion, have been presented as they relate to fashion.

The different AoF activities provide students with experience of top designers, and ease the process of developing relationships with other motivated fashion students from around the world.

What are some of the biggest changes that have occurred in fashion education over the past five (or ten) years?

Technology and access to the Internet have completely modified the vision and perception of what fashion is and the way people approach it. Globalization has changed the student population, and people come from everywhere to study in the United States. It brings an interesting melting pot of cultures, and adds to the creative dynamic of the classroom.

Marketing and branding have confused the luxury and fashion industries. Retailers have blurred the boundaries between fashion designer, product designer, and merchandiser, giving birth to a "fast fashion" phenomenon and a false sense of fashion democratization. Marketers also exploit the current concern for the environment and fair labor and trade laws to drive sales without any genuine effect.

Traditional universities are still dealing with an obsolete approach: apparel design, not fashion design. Educators are coming from these schools with little professional experience. It then becomes difficult for universities to hire technical professors.

New positions outside of design are emerging in the industry such as product design, trend forecasting, and press communication. For private schools, it has been a lucrative business because it multiplies career options. It is also easier to invest in computers and promote merchandising, for example, rather than fashion design, which requires professors with a vast knowledge in addition to good creative and technical skills.

Students also have many loans to pay back because of the cost of education in the United States that make it impossible for them to launch their own brand, unlike students in Europe. Once they finally make their way into the job market, they are asked to knock off designs and work on computer tasks, which is disappointing for such talented students.

A new challenge for the U.S. fashion industry and education would be the adoption of a copyright law for fashion design with the Design Piracy Prohibition Act. The act will push corporations to regulate their current standards of copyright in order to avoid any legislative action or negative publicity. The act will encourage them to invest and work with true designers rather than shopping for ideas. It will provide young professionals with access to the creative positions that they deserve and enable them to be recognized for their work. When the Design Piracy Prohibition Act passes, the United States could ride the crest of a new revolutionary fashion, fueled by the creative potential of their young designers. This will give the U.S. fashion industry a true future.

What are the primary elements one must possess to be a successful designer? How can students develop these successfully?

- Be patient, open minded, curious, and experimental.
- Have rigor, a passion for fashion, a vision, and a strategy.
- Have good basis in art, and strong knowledge in contemporary art, fashion culture, and history.
- Be articulate and able to communicate ideas through whatever the medium, and be able to work with others.
- Always be just in time.

Fashion is a discipline requiring a lot of abilities, skills, extensive knowledge, and assets. Therefore, a well-rounded education, dedication, and an indestructible willingness are key. Apprenticeship is very important. If we observe the path taken by the most influential designers, they have all worked under a master at one point in their developing careers. Nothing is more important for students than to be in contact with creative professional people to help lead them.

How do you define great fashion design?

- When all the technical aspects, from sewing, pattern drafting, draping, and finishing are perfect.
- When it is a new silhouette, something never seen, loaded with a sense of culture, art, and with philosophy and emotion.
- When it is conceptual but also contemporary.
- When it embellishes a woman by giving her more strength, shape, power, and confidence.
- When it has discrete charm, no ostentation, but with original aesthetics and modernity.

▷ **Master classes** AoF Foundation courses focus on the creative and conceptual process of designing fashion by stressing innovative form, material, and scale, so that future professionals advance fashion design.

interview: first steps

Lisa Smilor

Associate Executive Director, Council of Fashion Designers of America (CFDA)

Called the "Godmother of Fashion" by CFDA President Diane von Furstenberg, Lisa Smilor is a leading force in supporting fashion design education and students as they transition into burgeoning young professionals. Her years of working with fashion talent at both Parsons the New School for Design and, currently, The CFDA, gives her a solid understanding of how education and industry can best nurture and guide students.

▽ **Join the party** CFDA membership consists of more than 350 of America's foremost womenswear, menswear, jewelry, and accessory designers. This picture was taken at the 2008 New Member Party at Elie Tahari's home.

Can you describe your job and how it relates to education and/or fashion design?

I wear many hats, but my primary responsibilities include the development and overseeing of CFDA's Educational Initiatives, including but not limited to:

- CFDA/Teen Vogue Scholarship, in partnership with Target
- CFDA Scholarship Program
- Geoffrey Beene Fashion Scholar Award
- Liz Claiborne Design Scholarship
- CFDA/Vogue Fashion Fund

CFDA President Diane von Furstenberg refers to me as the "Godmother of Fashion"—there are very few emerging fashion designers who I have not assisted in my twenty-plus years working within the fashion industry. I have the unique opportunity to recognize and work closely with talented designers while they are still in school, and then to support their growth through the early years of their careers.

I work closely with the chairpersons and/or deans at the (sixteen) leading design colleges and universities in the United States and serve as adviser, critic, judge and/or selection committee member for various fashion design programs, initiatives, and organizations.

How has the fashion industry changed over the past five to seven years? How do these changes at the professional level create and inform shifts in education?

In the past decade, there has been a proliferation of talented (and smart, business-minded) younger designers who are being recognized early on by fashion editors, retailers, and financial investors. Mega-brands such as Ralph Lauren, Marc Jacobs, Donna Karan, Calvin Klein, and Michael Kors still have a strong presence on the selling floors and pages of the magazines, but there is a much greater opportunity for emerging designers to be noticed sooner than they might have in the past.

A designer's first steps are, therefore, now more important than ever. While in school, a design student should have various internships, but also make the time to shop stores and boutiques frequently, read trade papers regularly, etc. To have an awareness of what is selling, knowing what the experts are saying, will all be to a designer's advantage.

What are the hallmarks of "great" or "successful" fashion design?

A designer should have (and remain true to) their vision—a "signature" that remains a constant part of his/her design DNA. Great or successful designs are, in my opinion, a clever and thought-out balance of recognized familiarity with that designer's signature, combined with the element(s) of "pushing the envelope" to the next or newest level, representing an unexpected yet perfect solution to a season's "what's next" design question(s). When it's right, great design excites the consumer.

What changes will occur in the fashion industry over the next seven to ten years? What can students and young professionals do to prepare for these changes?

Good design will continue to be paramount, but there is an appreciation for value. Now, more than ever, an item should evoke a "must have" feeling for the consumer, combined with a special and/or unique quality that justifies the purchase.

There will also be more attention paid to the principles of supply and demand. The market has been oversaturated, and stores, designers, and consumers are all currently redefining the way business is done. Designers need to be keenly aware of how stores are buying, how and when their merchandise will hit the selling floor, how and when the consumer is buying, and make sure that each collection has pieces that will cover all the bases throughout the season.

How can students best make the transition from the classroom to the professional world?

Students should look for internships and/or jobs where they will have the opportunity to develop relationships with fabric mills, production facilities, shippers, editors, buyers, or anyone else who will help them navigate the early years of their career.

What is most successful about the fashion design community today? What areas need to be addressed more (by students, or industry, or professionals)?

Fashion has a life of its own, which is what makes it so exciting from season to season. What has worked or was popular in the past may no longer be valid. In my opinion, a key factor that has contributed to the success of the fashion industry has been the ability to shift, as necessary. Designers, editors, and retailers have been able to anticipate the next need, and deliver it to their customers.

▷ **Rewarding talent** The annual CFDA awards ceremony recognizes contributions to American fashion by individuals. *Top right*: CFDA President Diane von Furstenberg, who took the fashion world by storm with her iconic wrap dress, is a previous winner of the CFDA Lifetime Achievement Award. *Middle right*: Ralph Lauren, pictured here with his wife Ricky, was awarded the CFDA Popular Vote Award in 2009, through votes cast online by the public for their favorite designer. *Bottom right*: Sisters Kate and Laura Mulleavy of Rodarte fame won the Womenswear Designer of the Year Award, and here accompany actress Diane Kruger.

interview: inside the industry

Kat Nadj

UK Human Resources Manager for Gucci Group

With a corporate portfolio containing some of the world's most powerful brands such as Gucci, Alexander McQueen, and Stella McCartney, Gucci Group's Kat Nadj meets with prospective hires for the various design teams. Her exposure to top design talent has sharpened her views on what makes a successful portfolio, what leading design firms are seeking, and how students can best prepare for the professional market.

What is your professional affiliation and title? Can you describe your job and how it relates to education and/or fashion design?

I am the UK HR manager for Gucci Group. I manage recruitment from store level to design and corporate levels. I meet with a lot of design students from some of the best fashion schools in the world. When one of our brands needs an intern or an assistant designer, I call the schools with exact specifications (embroidery, pattern-cutting skills, etc.) and they send me a list of the students who fit the profile. More often, I meet with students on a much more speculative basis, as I like to understand the available talent out there for future reference.

I am lucky enough to have been asked to judge fashion competitions and final thesis reviews. It is here that I learn from creative experts the ways of understanding and appreciating fashion design in all its different forms, be it theoretically, conceptually, or commercially. I am constantly astounded at how amazingly talented the students are.

What are the hallmarks of a successful portfolio?

Having worked closely with design studios and fashion creatives, it is clear that the most important factor that contributes to a successful portfolio is seeing an idea transform into the design.

Research and sketches by hand are fundamental; I love seeing pencil to paper and how an idea can grow into something beautiful and wearable. Gucci Group has one of the most successful portfolios of brands in the world. What sets Gucci Group aside from the rest of its competitors is its unique composition of brands under one umbrella. As much as these brands complement each other, they are vastly different and therefore cater to all tastes, from classic to the fashion-forward.

How do you define "great" or "successful" fashion design?

The definition of successful fashion design depends on the perspective from which it is looked at. Some look at fashion from a purely commercial standpoint, where the most important elements are volume and turnover.

I believe that fashion design stems from an ability to be as creatively innovative as possible. I tend to overlook people who copy others: There is a fine line between being inspired and plagiarism. Take the more senior geniuses like Alaia and Gaultier and the younger ones like Nicolas Ghesquiere or Alexander McQueen—they are the masters of innovation, constantly striving to evolve and set trends instead of following them.

What changes will occur globally in the fashion industry over the next seven to ten years? What can students and young professionals do in order to prepare for these changes?

Nobody can say exactly what will happen, because nobody possesses a crystal ball. Nevertheless, I think that students must be aware of evolving consumers' attitudes. They have to be able to listen to the market and channel their creativity into something relevant. In the digital era, consumers talk to us all the time; we cannot ignore it anymore.

What are the industry and consumers looking for most today from the next generation of fashion designers?

The industry is continually looking for the next creative or pioneering design or designer, but at the same time these new ideas need to remain relevant to the here and now.

Consumers are followers of fashion, but today they are more savvy and demanding than ever. They love to buy what they see on celebrities and in the magazines, but at the same time they ask for continuous originality and want to be surprised and inspired.

▽ **Stella moments** Launching her own label shortly after graduating from Central Saint Martins, Stella McCartney has partnered with Gucci Group and also designs athleticwear for Adidas. An avid supporter for animal rights, she does not use animal products in her collections.

▷ **Top brass** Trained on Savile Row, McQueen launched his own line in 1994 and partnered Gucci Group in 1997. He has received the British Designer of the Year Award three times and his global empire includes womenswear, menswear, perfume, and eyewear.

UNIT 25
tools & supplies

As with any profession, having quality tools and materials will create quality work.

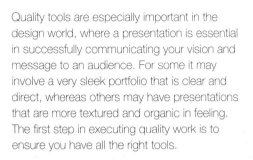

Quality tools are especially important in the design world, where a presentation is essential in successfully communicating your vision and message to an audience. For some it may involve a very sleek portfolio that is clear and direct, whereas others may have presentations that are more textured and organic in feeling. The first step in executing quality work is to ensure you have all the right tools.

Portfolio:
- Nonzipper type suggested, with ring-binder interior that allows for pages to be changed

Papers:
- 11 x 14 in. (28 x 35.5 cm) croquis sketchbook; a brand that takes wet and dry media well is suggested
- 11 x 14 in. (28 x 35.5 cm) pad of tracing paper

General:
- 18 x 2 in. (45 x 5 cm) transparent grid ruler
- 12 x 1 in. (30 x 2.5 cm) transparent grid ruler
- Paper scissors
- Double-stick tape
- Regular tape
- Rubber cement or glue stick
- Kneaded eraser
- Plastic white eraser
- Color-correct lamp; this has warm/cool bulbs for color-matching accuracy

Drawing pen

Drawing materials:
- Pencils of various grades; such as HB, 2B, 2H, etc.
- Mechanical pencil and leads
- Pencil sharpener
- Pigma Micron Pens (suggested brand) in sizes .08, .03, .005 for technical flats

Media:
- Marker set; brands such as Berol Prismacolor, Chartpak, Design Art Markers, Pantone Letraset are suggested
- Colored pencil set; 72-count suggested
- Extra white pencils
- Cold-pressed watercolor paper, cut to size to fit a portfolio of your choosing
- Brushes, such as Winsor & Newton Series 7 (7 and 2), or similar sable-hair brushes
- Paint palette with multiple wells

Mechanical pencil

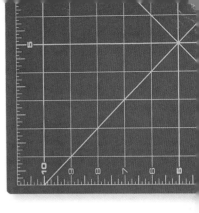

Supplies for 3D Work

Listed below are the primary tools you will need to begin most 3D design projects for protyping garments in muslin.

Muslin:
- Medium weight; 10 yards (9 m) is suggested

Seam ripper

Measuring tools:
- 60-in. (1.5-m) tape measure
- 18 or 24 x 2 in. (45 or 60 x 5 cm) clear plastic ruler, divided into ⅛-in. (3-mm) grids
- French curve
- 12 x 1 in. (30 x 2.5 cm) clear plastic ruler, divided into ⅛ in. (3 mm)
- Optional but useful: hip curve; yard stick; and L-square ruler

Cutting tools:
- Seam ripper
- Paper scissors
- Fabric scissors (shears)
- Cutting board
- Optional but useful: small scissors for clipping thread

Draping and patternmaking supplies:
- Black twill tape to mark dressform; 4–5 yards (3.7–4.6 m) to start
- Red and blue pencils to identify pattern changes
- Pattern paper (dotted paper for making patterns); 10 yards (9 m) to begin
- Muslin; 10 yards (9 m) to begin
- Pushpins; small package

Sewing tools and supplies:
- Straight pins; size 17 is suggested
- Bobbins and case for industrial sewing machines
- Hand-sewing needles; assorted sizes
- Pin cushion or pin dispenser
- Tracing wheel
- Carbon paper in blue and white
- Pattern-drafting spiked tracing wheel
- Chalk wheel
- Spools of thread
- White medium-weight fusible interfacing; one package, or 1 yard (0.9 m) is suggested
- 7-in. (18-cm) zippers for skirts
- 10–12-in. (25–30-cm) invisible zippers for dresses
- Assorted buttons

Chalk wheel and chalk

Gouache paints:

Illustrations must provide the viewer with an accurate depiction of color and fabric so that the collection can be successfully analyzed during the design phases. Gouache paint enables designers to match colors exactly and depict fabric textures and weights more successfully than other, flatter mediums. From sheer chiffons to highly dense and textured wools, gouache has a broad range of application, and can also be used with mixed media (such as marker and colored pencil) to accurately depict designs.

Gouache colors:

Alizarin crimson	Turquoise blue
Spectrum red	Ultramarine
Grenadine	Prussian blue
Bengal rose	Spectrum violet
Orange lake light	Burnt sienna
Naples yellow	Burnt umber
Spectrum yellow	Vandyke brown
Yellow ochre	Zinc white
Permanent green	Jet or lamp black
Middle olive green	
Cobalt blue	

Tracing wheel

Fabric scissors

Software

The application of software in fashion design is virtually limitless. From creating woven patterns, printed graphics, and technical "flat" drawings in production, to concept boards used in presentations, various types of software can make the design process effective and efficient. Here are just some of the more popular applications used by professional designers.

- **Adobe Photoshop** is a paint application (pixel based) used primarily for creating image and photograph manipulations, composites and collages, concept boards, color palettes, select textile designs, colorways for fabric designs, basic stripe and plaid layouts, digital flats, painterly effects, texture, and rendering for digital illustration.

- **Adobe Illustrator** is an object-oriented application (vector based) used primarily for creating graphics, logos, font-based designs, select textile designs, drawing and rendering of illustrative flats, digital fashion illustration, and page layouts.

- **Lectra U4ia** is a paint application specifically geared toward creating textile design colorways, repeats, texture mapping for illustration, and knitwear design.

Internet Resources

Conducting web-based research allows for efficient and diverse exposure, and can provide a solid foundation before advancing to other means of research such as printed material and museums. From researching designer runway shows, historical garments, global trends, and museum artifacts, the variety of sites can provide you with plenty of useful material.

www.firstview.com
One of the best sites for browsing a seemingly limitless amount of designer runway shows, most free of charge, some for cost. This site also sells videos of runway shows, books, and photos, and provides a calendar for forthcoming fashion events.

www.style.com
"The online home of *Vogue*" lets you view selected runway collections and runway videos online, free of charge. Information is also provided via blogging, trends and shopping, menswear coverage, and more.

www.vintagefashionguild.org
A rich resource for those interested in vintage fashion. Read about fashion history, view book reviews, learn how to date vintage finds, and use the blog with other aficionados.

www.hintmag.com
View collection highlights, read show reviews, keep up-to-date on fashion news and events, and stay connected to the "industry at large."

www.wgsn.com
A seemingly endless amount of information is offered about fashion around the world and the trends that shape the industry.

www.wwd.com
Through membership, Women's Wear Daily (WWD) offers daily and thorough coverage of the fashion industry around the globe. One of the best news resources for staying up-to-date.

www.fashion-era.com
The site for researching period fashion, offering extensive illustrations and text to contextualize each period.

www.fashion.about.com
From learning about style basics, reading blogs during fashion week, skimming Hollywood's "best dressed lists," shopping for fashion, and obtaining links for historical research, this site has it covered.

Index

Credits

Steven Faerm would like to thank:

Noel Palomo Lovinski for contributions to writing and research.
Elizabeth Morano for contributions to research.
Fiona Dieffenbacher for help on the knitwear section.
Emmanuel Laurent for the photograph of Nathalie Doucet.
Fiona Struengmann for the Anna Zwick photographs, pages 104–105.
Lizzy Oppenheimer for photography on pages 96–97 and 124.
Mike Devito, who shot most of the 2D student work and all of the Parsons runway shots.

Thank you to the following students whose work features in the book:

Bessie Afnaim, p51
Samantha Aprea, p71
Maria Castro, p54
Ivy Chen, p110, 120
Heesung Choi, p24, 92
Janne Chung, p41
Kristine Constantine, p131
Nicole Ferrada, p37
Robert Fitzsimmons, p23
Brian Franklin, p86, 89, 103
Angela Gao, p98
Yoon Jeong Gee, p50
Sarah Hermez, p55
Bora Hong, p42, 77
Wyatt Hough, p13, 27
Laura Jung, p112–113, 121
Elizabeth Kennedy, p22
Jiyup Kim, p108–109
Kyne Kim, p88, 94, 106
Lydia Kim, p92–93, 114–115
Min sun Kim, p25, 92–93, 94–95
Sylvia Kwan, cover drawings, p23, 25, 31, 33, 37, 45, 46, 52, 68–69, 80–85
Sarah Law, p44
Bobae Lee, p10–11, 64–65, 66, 117
HJ Lee, p38–39, 47, 73, 90–91
Nayeon Lee, p93

Christine Mayes, p35, 74–75, 79, 87
Cullen Meyers, p40
Keith Mosbacher, p9
Monica Noh, p67
Michelle Ochs, book cover collection
Georgiana Ortiz, p4–5, 57
Shawn Reddy, p7, 58, 76–77, 96–97, 122, 124
Andrew Rogers, p56
Jennifer Rubin, opening page, p6, 36, 65
Rachel Rymar, p41
Christine Samar, p50, 78–79
Wen Shi, p73, 86, 93, 118–119
Jigon Son, p72–73
Stephanie Suberville, p100–101
Brandon Sun, p43, 89
Nanae Takata, p8, 27, 31, 35, 38, 111, 123, 128
Nanette Thorne, p39
Eri Wakiyama, p9, 130
Atsuko Yagi, opening spread
Stephanie Yang, p48
Clara Yoo, p10, 55, 107, 123
Sonia Yoon, p70
Laura Zukaite, p27
Anna Zwick, p104–105

Quarto would like to thank the following agencies for kindly supplying images for inclusion in this book:

b = bottom; c = center; t = top; l = left; m = middle; r = right

Rex Features: p10bl, 16, 17, 18, 19, 21, 33b, 40bl, 43ct, 33cb, 45br, 47cl, 109ct, 137br&l; Alamy: p12bl, 41cr; Corbis: p13tl, 15t, 34, 72ct, 98tr

Clear Channel www.clearchannel.com

We would also like to thank the students at London College of Fashion who kindly allowed us to reproduce their work.

All other images are the copyright of Quarto Publishing plc. While every effort has been made to credit contributors, Quarto would like to apologize should there be any omissions or errors, and would be pleased to make the appropriate correction for future editions of the book.